BRANDING
UNBOUND

**THE FUTURE OF ADVERTISING, SALES,
AND THE BRAND EXPERIENCE IN THE WIRELESS AGE**

RICK MATHIESON

⁍AMACOM
AMERICAN MANAGEMENT ASSOCIATION
New York • Atlanta • Brussels • Chicago • Mexico City • San Francisco
Shanghai • Tokyo • Toronto • Washington, D.C.

This publication is designed to provide accurate and authoritative information in regard to the subject matter covered. It is sold with the understanding that the publisher is not engaged in rendering legal, accounting, or other professional service. If legal advice or other expert assistance is required, the services of a competent professional person should be sought.

Library of Congress Cataloging-in-Publication Data

Mathieson, Rick.
        Branding unbound : the future of advertising, sales, and the brand experience in the wireless age / Rick Mathieson.— 1st ed.
            p. cm.
        Includes bibliographical references and index.
        ISBN 0-8144-7287-7
        1. Mobile commerce.   2. Product management.   I. Title.

    HF5548.34.M38   2005
    658.8'72—dc22

                                                                          2005002544

Printing number

10   9   8   7   6   5   4   3   2   1

**FOR JUDY AND KATE,
MY REASONS**

Contents

Introduction

Advertising displays that call out to you on a first-name basis.

Services that let you shop for pizza, music, books, and movies—anywhere, anytime.

Stores where the costs of goods is automatically deducted from your bank account—without you ever writing a check, doling out cash, swiping a card, or standing in line.

And commercials broadcast so only you can hear them—seemingly from inside your own head.

MARKETING'S WIRELESS FUTURE IS HERE. READY TO MAKE THE MOST OF IT?

It turns out that the Internet was just a warm-up act. A decade ago, the Internet hype machine pitched the World Wide Web as a marketer's dream come true—an interactive, one-to-one utopia, linking shoppers and their quarry in the electronically enabled Elysium Fields of 24-7 commerce.

Of course, Google, Amazon, and eBay notwithstanding, banner ads, online "communities of interest," and click-and-mortar "e-tailing" have yet to truly deliver the eyeballs, interest, or sales they promised—tethered as they've been to a cumbersome, confounding device called the desktop PC.

Now, all that's changing. A new generation of wireless Internet technology is finally liberating the Net from its deskbound subjugation. Thanks to new wireless devices and high-speed mobile networks, the Information Superhighway and its advertising "billboards," applications, and services are finally hitting the road with you. Along the way, they're delivering on two tenets, heretofore unfulfilled, that are central to the Internet's promise. The first: anywhere. The second: anytime.

Today, there are over 1.7 billion Internet-enabled cell phones worldwide, allowing users to browse the Web, take pictures, send e-mail, watch TV, play games, and yes, even talk.[1] By 2007, there will be a billion more—one for every three people on the planet— each sporting computing power that rivals that of NASA's original Apollo space program.[2, 3] Meanwhile, nearly 600 million wireless-enabled laptop computers, PDAs, and "smart phones" (cell phone / PDA hybrids) feature new forms of wireless connectivity—"wireless fidelity" (Wi-Fi), ultra-wideband, Bluetooth, and "third generation" (3G) cellular, among others—many only now becoming familiar to the average consumer.[4] Factor in emerging new fuel-cell batteries that will untether devices for longer and longer periods of time and, say experts, these whole new levels of connectivity and computing power will fundamentally redefine how—and where— people live, work, learn, and play.

"This confluence of technologies is really unprecedented in the short history of electronic technology," says Gene Becker, program director for the Mobile and Media Systems Lab at Hewlett-Packard. "The end result is a lot of opportunity for innovation and experimentation in the ways that people use this stuff. Clearly the mobile experience is going to be one of them that is transformed quite extraordinarily."*

In fact, it has already begun.

FROM HERE TO UBIQUITY

To most marketers outside Japan, the word DoCoMo may still evoke the name of a particularly unfortunate Beach Boys song. But to the world's high-tech digirati, the name of Japan's dominant mobile services carrier has long been synonymous for high-speed, high-bandwidth, high-octane wireless innovation.

Train-bound Japanese commuters watch TV, play games, and shop from their 3G-enabled NTT DoCoMo *i-mode* handsets. *Keiti* (handset)–crazed teenagers videoconference with their far-flung *tomodachi*. And a society short on landline Internet connections, and shorter on personal living space, has embraced the Internet—many without ever logging on to a PC.

Seven hundred fifteen miles to the northeast, wireless is the rage for 34 million South Koreans who use their cell phones to do everything from making purchases, to trading securities, to checking closed-circuit traffic cameras before making the trip home. In 2004, 500 Korean families moved into homes wired with Samsung's "hometiva" technology.[5] Using a tablet-like "Home Pad" or a cell phone, they can call up a movie to their plasma screen TVs, brew coffee, or even tap into surveillance cameras to monitor for prowlers. By 2007, Korea's Ministry of Information and Communications hopes to expand this level of connectivity to over 10 million households.[6]

Meanwhile, from Manila to Helsinki to London, teenagers use cell phones, pagers, and PDAs to send text messages, also called SMS for "short message services," to coordinate protests, to stage

*Note: Quotations without sources come from interviews conducted specifically for *Branding Unbound*; those with sources are from the author's previously published work or from the sources specified.

raves, or simply to connect with friends in what techno-anthropologist Howard Rheingold famously described as "Thumb Tribes."

The craze even has its first malady—a condition called "Texter's Thumb," a form of tenosynovitis that causes inflammation of the tendons that snake along the hand and wrist due to pecking out excessive numbers of messages.[7]

In 2006, consumers will send an estimated 700 billion text messages worldwide, according to industry trade group GSM Association. And as mobile IM, or Instant Messaging via cell phones, proliferates, the number of messages could prove quite staggering.

These same sorts of technologies are taking off in the United States.

Over 40 million Americans actively use text messaging, including 57 percent of all eighteen- to twenty-five-year-old mobile subscribers, according to mobile marketing firm Enpocket.[8] Over 13.5 million people regularly send text messages to vote for contestants on Fox-TV's *American Idol* talent show.[9] And American cell phone subscribers are spending nearly $250 million to download the latest hit music-clip "ringtone."[10]

But this digital revolution is much, much more than just Internet-enabled handsets, music downloads, and SMS–wielding adolescents. Increasingly, it's about everyday products being embedded with ubiquitous, "always-on" wireless connectivity and intelligence.

The OnStar service in your car, for instance, uses global positioning system (GPS) technologies to pinpoint your location with an accuracy of within ten meters, gives you verbal directions to your next destination, unlocks your door if your toddler locks himself in with the keys, and calls 911 if your airbags are deployed in a crash. Similar GPS technologies in "Personal Locator Devices," like those from Wherify, can help you monitor your child's every move from a secure Web site, and alert you if Johnny doesn't make his 3 P.M. piano lesson or if Sally ventures too far from the neighborhood. The Bluetooth connection in your digital camera transmits the pictures from Mom's birthday party to the nearest desktop printer. The Wi-Fi–based Apple Airport Express hub connected to your home computer broadcasts your collection of Maroon 5 MP3s from any stereo system in the house. And the radio frequency identification (RFID)–based transponder affixed to your car electronically pays for toll roads and bridges without you ever having to let up on the accelerator.

As 3G cellular networks begin to proliferate here, they will enable unified voice, video, and data connections that let you use your mobile phone to videoconference your kids and see how they're doing—quite literally. Soon, "smart clothes" will routinely monitor heart patients and alert doctors to impending heart attacks.[11] Tiny "smart dust" sensors, less than one hundred cubic millimeters in size, will monitor the nation's food supply for chemical and biological agents—and provide video, audio, and troop movement analysis on the battlefield. And projects like Korea's Smart Home initiative presage an age of intelligent homes, buildings, and stores that react to your every command, or offer you up services and goods based on your personal preferences.[12]

Yet for all the frissons these possibilities may inspire, the second chapter of the Internet is quite different from the first. Hobbled by the dot-com implosion and hyperlink-inspired hyperbole, the Internet's emerging wireless era is predicated on using practical, inexpensive technology to simply extend proven business solutions from the virtual world into the real one.

And while wireless has many applications, from health care, to defense, to supply chain management, to education, the impact may be most profound and promising—and perilous—for those at the front lines of twenty-first-century business: marketers.

THE BURGER KING SYNDROME

Already, the convergence of high-speed networks and new digital devices is dramatically reshaping the cultural and media landscapes.

A generation weaned on TiVo, video on demand (VOD), chat rooms, and instant messaging has grown accustomed to living seamlessly and simultaneously on- and offline. American teens and twenty-somethings are gravitating to new "social networking" services like Dodgeball, which lets them send text messages to alert friends of their current whereabouts so they can meet up, make plans, or just get their gossip on.

Managers surf the Web while trapped in interminable meetings. Moms call home while standing in line for groceries. We've all grown accustomed to time-shifting our consumption of media— watching our favorite TV shows when we get a spare moment, instead of the second they're broadcast. And we're increasingly skipping the advertising all together.

Part of this change is the direct result of the sheer multitude of entertainment choices afforded by digital technology. Thirty-seven percent of Americans say they watch less television due to online activities, according to a report on broadband Internet usage by the Pew Internet and American Life Project.[13]

"Twelve years ago, you could reach 50 percent of the American audience with three TV spots, and today, it takes seventy," says Chuck Porter, a founder of Miami-based advertising powerhouse Crispin Porter + Bogusky (CPB). "Media fragmentation has absolutely forced advertisers to rethink the way to build brands."

Indeed, according to one controversial report from Nielsen Media Research, there are indications that up to 13 percent of one of America's most important cohorts, the young male audience, has abandoned network television in recent years—lost, presumably, to cable, the Internet, and video games.[14]

Ah, those video games: By some estimates, they now score over $11 billion a year. That's more than Hollywood makes at the U.S. box office.[15] Since 1997, the compound annual growth rate in the number of consumers playing video games has topped 14 percent, while watching television and cable has grown only 1.9 percent.[16] As you might imagine, the entire gaming segment is heading into hyperdrive as games go mobile—a burgeoning segment that will top $1 billion in the United States by 2008, according to IDC analyst Lewis Ward.

And it's not just first-person shooter games for young male punks. In the United States, women 18 and older now make up 40 percent of all Internet gamers, and 58 percent of all mobile gamers.[17, 18] Women of all ages are turning to the Internet, both wireline and wireless—accounting for 60 percent of all online purchases, according to Nielsen/NetRatings.

Meanwhile, 69 percent of consumers express interest in ad-skipping technologies like TiVo and other digital video recorders (DVRs).[19] Nearly 33.5 million households will adopt the technology by the end of 2008—up dramatically from 7 million homes in early 2005, according to research firm Yankee Group.[20] And new hand-held versions, like Microsoft's Media2Go and movies-music-gaming "media center" versions of the Sony PSP and the VIA Eve console, are increasingly popular.

Combine this trend with new satellite-based broadband TV/Internet/phone networks like those from Clearwire and WildBlue, and peer-to-peer networks like Kazaa, Grokster, and eDonkey, and suddenly, content of all kinds—digital TV, movies, music, games, photos, personal information, shopping, and more—takes on a level of portability, accessibility, and personalization previously unimaginable.

Armed and wireless, the most unsatisfied members of our consumer republic will increasingly reject media that fail to meet their interests and increasingly mobile, interconnected lifestyles. Others will enhance their television, radio, and print experiences with the kind of instant, personalized interactivity no other medium can provide.

Like the Burger King commercials of yore, the only rule that matters in this increasingly fragmented mediascape is as simple as it is powerful: Now more than ever, it's your way, or no way at all.

For Madison Avenue, this means change is, quite literally, in the air.

"The creative community is still fixated with thirty-second commercials, and the clock is ticking," Coca-Cola president Chuck Fruit recently declared, adding that brands like Coke spend roughly three-fourths of their ad budgets on television. "That percentage will go down steadily for the next decade to well under half."[21]

At issue: accountability. As clients demand more than just brand exposure, the advertising industry finds itself gravitating toward so-called "performance-based" campaigns, pumping over $10 billion into imminently measurable media. These include venues such as the Internet and emerging forms of "on-demand advertising" that enable consumers to click through for product information via DVRs and other set-top interactive television technologies.

According to Forrester Research, marketers are already investing nearly $1 billion into the most measurable, personal, and direct link to consumers ever devised: wireless.[22]

"For the first time ever, brands have the ability to have meaningful interactions with consumers that beat all other media in terms of both breadth and frequency," says John Ricketts, a strategy director for Ogilvy Asia/Pacific, which has created numerous mobile marketing initiatives for the likes of Unilever's Lipton's Tea, Northwest Airlines, and Nestlé. Through two-way wireless communications via SMS and wireless Web sites, "everything in the physical world suddenly becomes interactive," he says. "Television becomes interactive. Outdoor signage becomes interactive. Point of sale becomes interactive. Even the product itself becomes an invitation to have an interaction and bring value to consumers that is really quite unprecedented."

Still, for many marketers and their advertising agencies, wireless represents a mysterious and challenging new component of the marketing mix.

"There are a lot of people who have gotten really good at making television commercials and very, very good at buying traditional media," says CPB's Porter, whose agency has made a name for itself by capitalizing on decidedly nontraditional advertising venues—most notably with its "Subservient Chicken" interactive online game for Burger King, which was accessed by over 250 million people worldwide. "When they look at this changing media space, there's a reluctance to say, 'Holy shit, we have to change everything.' But marketers had better start embracing other media—including wireless—or they're going to discover their customers have hit the snooze button."

WINNING WITHOUT WIRES

From McDonald's to Starbucks to MTV to Procter & Gamble to Wal-Mart to Prada and beyond, some of today's top marketers are rising to the challenge—turning to new wireless technologies to create unprecedented differentiation, convenience, and loyalty.

We're not just talking about sales pitches sent to cell phones. It's far more than that. Today, companies of all sizes are using a host of new technologies to enable intelligent, wirelessly connected retail environments, communications, and services that are transforming the way consumers experience—and interact with—their favorite brands.

This book is designed to offer you an inside look at some of the most ingenious strategies these and other marketers are using to reach out and touch consumers in amazing new ways.

First, I'll provide an easy-to-understand field guide to the wireless landscape, one that will help even the most technophobic marketer understand the five key advantages of "mBranding," a term I use to describe the creation of competitive differentiation through wireless/mobile technologies. I hope to demystify the geek-speak behind the technology, and have included a glossary at the end of the book for easy reference.

Next, I'll give you an inside look at how marketers and their partners are putting these solutions to good use. You'll discover how:

▶ Marketers at Procter & Gamble, Unilever, McDonald's, Warner Brothers, Dunkin' Donuts, MasterCard, and Coca-Cola use the fusion of online, offline, and wireless advertising to boost the effectiveness of television, print, and radio campaigns upward of 15 percent.

▶ MTV, Fox-TV, HBO, Kellogg's, Comedy Central, and Discovery rely on the wireless platform to build unbreakable relationships in ways that put the traditional Internet to shame.

▶ E*TRADE, AOL Moviefone, eBay, Delta Airlines, Subway, Major League Baseball, and others make the most of new forms of "m-commerce"—the ability to buy and sell services and products anywhere, anytime.

▶ Suzuki, Pepsi, Yahoo, DaimlerChrysler, Time Warner, Universal, Disney, and Nike extend their branding power to new wireless content, applications, and games aimed at the eighteen- to thirty five-year-old hipsters these advertisers covet most.

▶ Prada, Metro AG, Wal-Mart, Borders, and Starbucks use wireless to enhance the actual in-store shopping experience to astonishing effect. See how new applications enable store clerks to offer you products based on past purchase behavior, and electronic transaction technologies that let you throw goods into your cart and walk out the door without ever writing a check, digging for cash, swiping a card—or standing in line.

▶ The Venetian Hotel, The Four Seasons, Carlson Hospitality, Disney World, and a growing number of other hotels, restaurants, and amusement parks create transparent, "pervasive" computing environments that anticipate your every need and ensure prompt—even preemptive—service that will redefine the guest experience for an entire generation of leisure and business travelers.

Later on, I'll show you how many of the 150 million camera phones in use today are being used in such phenomena as "moblogging" (public Web diaries and photo galleries posted by enthusiasts on the go), and collective acts of weirdness known as "flash mobs"—and what they mean to our notions of viral marketing. You'll discover emerging branded applications that sound like the stuff of science fiction: Designer clothes that tell the washing machine, "Don't wash me, I'm dry clean only." And, perhaps a bit more frightening, commercials, broadcast so only you can hear them, seemingly emanating from within your own head.

Along the way, I'll share insights from some of today's top marketers and thought leaders, such as Tom Peters, Don Peppers, and

Seth Godin, as they ruminate on how all this technology will enhance the brand experience.

Finally, I'll explore the world of marketing in the year 2020, including the mind-boggling ethical and business challenges marketers will face when everything you can access, anywhere, anytime, also has access to you.

Make no mistake, marketing's wireless revolution is real. By 2007, wireless innovations are expected to help generate $33 billion in new revenues for the companies that capitalize on them, according to research firm Allied Business Intelligence.[23] As they continue to untether the Internet, these new technologies herald massive opportunities for marketers who judiciously use their power to transform everything from advertising to retailing to customer care—and monumental challenges for those who fall behind.

TALKING 'BOUT A REVOLUTION

Wireless. It's not just for nerds anymore.

A Cheat Sheet

3G	Stands for the "Third Generation" of mobile phone technology. Fifty times faster than present-day cellular phone networks, delivers data at 144 kilobits per second—which is essential for video, music, Internet access, and more.
Wi-Fi	Stands for "Wireless Fidelity." An increasingly popular way to connect devices—PCs, printers, TVs—to the Net, and to each other, within a range of up to 300 feet.
Hot Spot	An area where Wi-Fi service is available so you can wirelessly connect to

	the Internet; frequently offered in cafés, airports, and hotels.
Mobile-Fi	Next-generation technology that extends high-speed wireless access to moving vehicles.
Bluetooth	With a range of about thirty feet, used to connect PCs to mobile phones or printers, and earpieces to phones.
WiMax	Long-distance Wi-Fi; can blanket areas more than a mile in radius to bring high-speed Internet access to homes and buildings too remote for traditional access.
Ultra-Wideband	Connects your favorite toys—PCs, video cameras, stereos, TV sets, TiVo—at speeds 500 times faster than Bluetooth, and fifty times faster than Wi-Fi.
GPS	The Global Positioning System, a constellation of twenty-four satellites that provides highly accurate data on a device's location; used extensively in car navigation solutions, and increasingly, for monitoring the location of children and elderly parents.
RFID	Radio Frequency Identification. Small RFID "smart tags" are tiny silicon chips that store data and a miniature antenna that enables the tag to communicate with networks. Could one day enable milk cartons that tell the store (or your refrigerator) that they're about to expire; lost TV re-

mote controls that can reach you through your Web browser to tell you where to find them, and much more.

ZigBee   "Smart dust" technology that coordinates communications among thousands of tiny sensors, each about the size of a coin. Could one day be used for managing a home, store, or office environment based on the occupants' preferences, for monitoring the toxicity of drinking water, and for controlling remote diagnostics of home appliances, cars, and even humans.

Java/BREW   Technologies for delivering and displaying content to mobile phones.

SMS   Stands for Short Message Service; basically e-mail for mobile phones. Synonymous with "texting" and "text messaging."

Mobile IM   Instant messaging, which offers real-time messaging with buddy lists, is increasingly being extended from the desktop Internet to the mobile world.

MMS   Multimedia Messaging. The successor of SMS; enables messages with text, pictures, graphics, sounds, and video.

WAP   Wireless Application Protocol; a standard for accessing the Web from mobile devices. A WAP site is a wireless Web site.

CHAPTER ONE

The Rise of mBranding

If today is like most others, Darla Marcomb will spend a few leisurely hours gazing out at the sparkling ocean from one of eighteen bay windows in her sprawling seaside home.

But Marcomb, a controller for a San Francisco–area HMO, hasn't exactly scored a palatial view of the Pacific from some pricey Bay-area mansion. Instead, her diversion is of the digital kind—perched within an astonishing online world simply known as *There*.

"I make the analogy that *There* is like an online Club Med," she says. "It's a place where you can go and do as little, or as much, as you want."

At its most essential, *There* is an Internet chat room with an eye-popping twist: A visually rich, 3D virtual environment—a bucolic island motif—that is akin to immersing oneself in some Gen-Y fantasy of Disney-does-Hedonism-on-the-South Pacific.

There's members select and customize so-called "avatars"— sophisticated cartoon character representations of themselves. They then proceed to race hover boards, fly jetpacks, play volleyball, explore a 6,000-kilometer world nearly the scale of Earth, or simply hang out and chat with family and friends.

Type in what you want to say, and text chat appears in comic book–style word balloons above your onscreen character's head. In an especially appealing bit of creative flair, "emoticons"—the emotive keystrokes ubiquitous in e-mail and instant messaging conversations—are instantly translated into your character's facial expressions.

The brainchild of former Electronic Arts wunderkind Will Harvey, *There* was launched after five years of development and over $37 million in investment capital from folks like Trip Hawkins, founder of Electronic Arts and mobile entertainment firm Digital Chocolate, and Jane Metcalfe and Louis Rosetto, cofounders of *Wired* magazine. Beyond the visual impact of this world, *There* is built from the ground up to help its members feed another fundamental human drive—the desire to make money.

Harvey and his team worked with an IMF economist to develop a working, laissez-faire economy based on Therebucks, a faux currency that members can buy for real dollars, with a conversion rate of something like 1,500 Therebucks per $1.

Buy a pair of virtual Levi's jeans, and your character's hipness quotient goes up. Buy a pair of virtual Nike AirMax shoes, and your character suddenly runs faster. It's addicting: In her first nine months as a subscriber, Marcomb says she spent over $1,100 very real dollars to rent and furnish her house, and to buy clothes, hairdos, and other products for her avatar. "I'm really into fashion," she says. "And I really like to shop."

Like the half-dozen other online virtual worlds that have hit the Internet since the early 1990s, *There* is based on an amazing concept. Using an Internet connection, you, your friend in New York, your uncle in St. Louis, and your brother in Sydney can log on and play chess, chat by a campfire, even conduct business, while jacked into virtual versions of your real-world selves from anywhere on earth. It's the *Matrix* without the lame dialogue.

"It's a way for people to create meaningful relationships with other people—and have a lot of fun together—even though they aren't geographically nearby," explains Marcomb.

Of course, in a conversation about wireless, that notion will take on new meaning in an emerging anywhere, anytime world where we will one day be able to access such virtual worlds from mobile devices.

But *There* is far more than just that. Because what Marcomb and other members may not realize is that for all its amazing features, the imaginary world of *There* offers a very real glimpse of the future of wireless that will be of great interest even to those who couldn't give a hoot about the virtual worlds of avatars and hover boards.

A BOOM WITH A VIEW

It's the sunglasses. When you're in *There*, you (as the invisible hand behind your character) use the computer screen built into your character's sunglasses to instantly access a pervasive, always-on, global "wireless" network.

Once "logged on," you can toggle between *There's* "real world" and its "wireless Internet." You can check your buddy list to see where your friends are, conduct transactions, join chat clubs, read news reports, view personal ads, rent dune buggies, place bids in auctions, and do an endless array of daily tasks from the beach, the back roads, or even above the clouds.

"The moment you see something you want, as instantly as the click of a button, it's yours," says Joe Laszlo, a senior analyst with Jupiter Research who has spent time in *There*. "That kind of instant gratification may well start to translate to the real world over the next couple of years as people get used to carrying around always-on data connections." See Figures 1-1 and 1-2.

In our own real world, that's what wireless is all about: empowering the user to interact—and transact—with people, places, even things via the most personal of devices.

The late Michael Dertouzos, director of MIT's Laboratory for Computer Science, once explained to me that tricked-out glasses could very well be a popular mechanism by which we augment our experience of reality. Charmed Technologies is working on a host of such "wearable computing" devices, including glasses, necklaces,

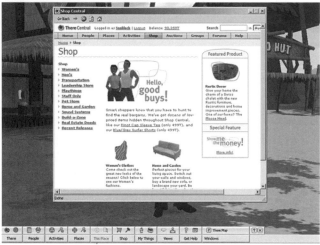

Figures 1-1 and 1-2. The 3D online world known as There offers a glimpse of a future where we can instantly toggle between the real world and a global, wireless Internet. Images courtesy of Forterra Systems.

and wristwatches. Its first product: a conference badge that records the contact information of other "CharmBadge" wearers as they come into range, and relays the information to an Internet portal for later review. Meanwhile, Ars Electronica Futurelab in Linz, Austria, is even working on "smart glasses" for automobile windshields, called Information and Navigation Systems Through Augmented Reality (INSTAR).[1] Designed to offer location-based information on nearby restaurants, hotels, gas stations, and other attractions, INSTAR will even give directions to the desired destination as you drive the interstate.

These are just a few of the possibilities. In his 1997 book, *What Will Be*, Dertouzos predicted that within this century, all sort of networks will work seamlessly together, and we'll all employ "BodyNets"—technology that provides an always-on mobile connection no matter where we go, via smart glasses or other devices. We'll check e-mail and exchange personal contact information and even multimedia with our friends and colleagues while on the go; place transactions without ever reaching for a wallet or purse; and look like lunatics as we walk down the street jabbering away on hands-free phone calls.

"Seamless mobility . . . that's where we think the future is headed," is how Motorola chief technology officer Padmasree Warrior put it at a recent conference called AlwaysOn at Stanford University.[2]

Today, that vision is still a ways off (except for the part about looking like a fool on a hands-free call). And it remains to be seen what forms it all will take.

The cell phone or PDA, as we know them today, may go away, morph into whole new forms, or just get smaller and more functional.

The Canesta Projection Keyboard, for instance, turns any mobile device into a virtual computer by using a tiny pattern projector to create the image of a full-size keyboard on a flat surface in front of a cell phone or PDA. The technology can read your finger movements as you "type" on the projected keyboard in real-time—making e-mail, Web surfing, and other data-intensive applications more portable than ever, while creating whole new roles for these devices. A new breed of sub-sub notebooks like the FlipStart PC from Paul Allen's Vulcan Ventures feature full PC functionality, powerful processors, and Wi-Fi connectivity in a compact device with a folding keyboard. Toshiba and others are rolling out wristwatch PDAs. And devices with larger screens and mini "qwerty" keyboards like the BlackBerry from RIM and the Hiptop from Danger have long been popular, as have hybrids from palmOne and Hewlett-Packard.

Regardless of the form, the combination of these devices, services, and emerging wireless networks mean the day of the "Body-Net" is coming—one that gives us access to a whole new world of services and capabilities.

MOBILE MARVELS

Some new services will be driven by type-based data entry. Craving a Steak Burrito Dos Manos with extra salsa from Baja Fresh? Already, cell phone users in Washington, D.C., can enter a short code on their cell phones, and 650 calories worth of gut-busting goodness will be waiting for them at the store's no-cash, no-wait line.

Other services will be based on sound. Hear a song you like on TV or the radio? Today, AT&T Wireless subscribers can hit #43 on their cell phones, hold their handsets up to the speaker, and within seconds, they'll receive the name of the artist and song so they can track it down for purchase.

Still other services will use that original human interface—the voice—to open up whole new possibilities. Novel solutions from Nuance, TellMe, and others already enable consumers to use virtually any cell phone to interface with computer systems and services that respond back in a human-like voice—complete with distinct personas, accents, and back stories. Delta Airline's low-cost carrier, Song, uses such voice-recognition technology to power its 1-800-FLYSONG service. Customers can make reservations by interfacing with an idiosyncratic, computerized voice that makes quips and comments based on the airline's fresh, cool brand identity.

"A few years from now, the phone call is going to be the lowest piece on the food chain," says Kenny Hirschorn, the director of strategy, imagineering, and futurology for U.K.–based mobile carrier Orange, one of the many companies working on creating this wireless future. "Of course, we will still facilitate voice communication. But on a daily basis, we will also awaken you in the morning. We will read you your e-mail. We will start the oven. We will arrange your transportation to and from wherever you want to go.

At the office, we will provide you with information and news. We will translate information into foreign languages, or translate information into your language for you. We will track your health. We will track the location of your family members, if that's what you want. We'll be your bank. We'll proactively order the groceries. We'll provide you entertainment and customized news. And we'll even watch your home when you sleep at night, because we will be jacked in to the security system. Very little of that has anything to do with making a telephone call."[3]

That's not to say that the cell phone will necessarily become our universal, movies-music-games-communications device for these kinds of services.

More likely, new products and services will deliver different types of content and applications to different devices and appliances: digital music to your car, movies from your PC to any plasma screen (or even any wall) in the house, games and even e-mail to your Nokia N-Gage handset or wireless Game Boy, software upgrades to your refrigerator or dishwasher.

You may control many of these services from your handheld or from a traditional Web portal. Other emerging technologies, like machine-to-machine (M2M) solutions, may deliver these services to any number of devices based on preset preferences, automatically as they become available.

Even in the here and now, cell phones, PDAs, and wireless-enabled laptops grow smaller, lighter, and more powerful by the day, linking to newfangled networks that are rapidly creating a mesh of Web technologies that extend the Internet, with apologies to Visa, "everywhere you want to be."

And most marketers have no idea what to do with it.

What does wireless mean to businesses trying to keep up with—and serve—the increasingly mobile masses? What happens when eyeballs we once aggregated by "gross ratings points" and "mass markets" now gather in micromarkets and "niches of one"? How do we redefine "advertising" and the "brand experience" when the most direct link to the consumer is less and less the 52-inch flat screen television in the living room, or the 17-inch PC monitor in the den or office, and more and more the completely personal, interactive device in the hands of virtually every man, woman, and child?

To chart a course in this amazing new world, we must first get a lay of the land—and the advantages the mobile milieu brings to marketers.

MBRANDING: A DEFINITION

Ask ten marketers to define the term "branding," and you're likely to get as many different answers. In fact, according to advertising giant Interbrand, the term has many possible meanings. From a legal perspective, branding can denote intellectual property. In terms of business valuation, branding can be perceived as the potential for future earnings. For marketers, it can run the gamut from the communication of a mixture of attributes, to a logo or symbol, to a "promise" or emotional compact between a consumer and a company that "creates influence or value for stakeholders"—to all of the above and more.[4]

For the purposes of this discussion, branding is the means by which a company creates a compelling consumer experience that differentiates the company's offerings from the competition, generates sales, and/or creates an emotional bond with customers. These experiences occur in exposure to retail environments, advertising, Web marketing, public relations, and person-to-person sales. With the advent of wireless/mobile technologies (terms that I will use interchangeably), our ability to create branded experiences now extends out from the TV and the PC screen to the so-called third screen of your handheld device. It even extends transparently, independent of any consumer device, to environments where company employees use always-on technology to better serve you, sometimes without you ever recognizing its use.

I call all of this "mBranding"—using the mobile medium to create differentiation, generate sales, and build customer loyalty as never before possible. If used correctly, it has five key advantages over virtually every other medium today.

IMMEDIACY

With wireless, there's no reason for consumers to ever again have to try to remember a URL the next time they find their way to a PC, much less try to recall a phone number or address.

Now, consumers can use their cell phones to enter a promotional four- to five-digit "short code" featured in a print, outdoor, or broadcast advertisement, right at the point of impression. Via SMS, they can have information sent to their e-mail address, or immediately participate in the promotion.

"Wireless really is more of a response device than it is a device for marketers to push out mass communications," says Jim Nail, a senior analyst for Forrester Research.

Sometimes, your phone becomes part of the promotion.

When Yahoo set out to promote the relaunch of its automotive site, autos.yahoo.com, the company worked with ad agency R/GA to create an electronic LED display that enabled pedestrians to play a giant, interactive video game, broadcast on part of the twenty-three-story Reuters sign in Times Square, via their cell phones. Pedestrians could call a number listed on the sign and queue up to play a forty-five-second Grand Prix–style auto racing game on a 7,000-square-foot screen, against each other or a computer. See Figure 1-3.

According to John Mayo-Smith, R/GA's vice president of technology, nearly 3,000 pedestrians participated in the promotion—nearly one player every minute of the 3,500 minutes the game was available. And the publicity generated by this feat of innovation exposed the initiative to millions around the world. "Show me another kind of channel where you can make that kind of impression," says Mayo-Smith.

MasterCard International capitalized on this same kind of immediacy to promote the use of its credit cards during the 2004 soccer championships in Portugal. Every time a consumer used a MasterCard to make a purchase at thirty-seven participating retailers around Lisbon and Oporto, the cardholder received a single-use short code that the holder could then enter into his or her cell phone for a chance to win instant cash prizes in-store. Winners

Figure 1-3. This digital billboard promoting Yahoo's auto site enabled nearly 3,000 pedestrians to use their cell phones to compete in a Grand Prix–style auto racing videogame on a 7,000-square-foot screen. Photo: R/GA.

received an instantaneous, real-time text message of any winnings and were automatically entered for a weekly drawing with prizes that included tickets to Euro 2004 matches and dinner with Portuguese soccer superstar Eusébio.

Another model: beaming. Several companies have been experimenting with the use of billboards and displays that can "beam" information to PDAs and cell phones via the devices' infrared or Bluetooth ports. Simon & Schuster has experimented with using the technology to send book excerpts to users who request them by holding their PDAs in front of outdoor signage for about seven seconds. And members of Equinox, the popular New York–based health club chain, can get information on class schedules and training options, as well as special promotions and incentives, beamed to their handhelds.

Newer camera phones are being used to enable the next generation of beaming using symbols called SpotCodes—black-and-white concentric rings printed on displays. Focusing the camera phone at the code and clicking any button launches a wireless service—product information sent to your e-mail address, or the ability to purchase an airplane ticket, for instance. In one model, you can walk into a Barnes & Noble, wave the phone at a book, and view comparison prices at Amazon.com.[5] Such applications have grown increasingly popular in Japan over the last few years, and you're bound to see them come to the United States with the next wave of camera phone technology.

Then there are actual transactions. While traditional media—TV, radio, and print—are excellent at creating awareness and preference, wireless can create immediate action.

In many parts of Europe, customers can buy sodas from vending machines by dialing a phone number on their cell phones. At the signal, the vending machine automatically drops the selected can of soda, and the charge shows up on the customer's next phone bill.

In Japan, Sony and DoCoMo have rolled out "smart card" technology that is embedded in certain cell phone models and is designed to store money or credit card information. At A.M./P.M. minimarts, All Nippon Airways, and thirty-seven other retailers and service providers, consumers can wave the phone at sensors at the cash register to deduct the amount of a purchase directly from their debit or credit account.[6]

We'll discuss more on this later, as well as how McDonald's, the Extra Future Store, Stop & Shop, and other stores have all been experimenting with other less complicated technologies to enable cashless transactions at the wave of an RFID–based key fob.

INTIMACY

Wireless devices are by far the most personal consumer appliances—much more than a desktop PC. After all, a family of four may have to share the PC in the den. But nowadays, everyone, down to the 10-year-old, has his or her own cell phone. And, to a person, we all share one mind-set: My device is irrefutably, undeniably, incontrovertibly *mine*. It comes with me everywhere I go. And only family, friends, and select others will be given access to our cell phone numbers. Don't call us, we'll call you.

For marketers, this has many effects. For starters, it creates tremendous pressure to respect consumer privacy. But it also provides opportunities to offer branded content and applications unique to an individual based on who they are, what they're doing, and where they're doing it.

In the United States, the popular Vindigo City Guide, a kind of Google for the physical world, is a PDA– and cell phone–based service covering seventy U.S. cities. Vindigo enables subscribers to find the best places to eat, shop, and hang out in their immediate vicinity. Advertisers are able to use the larger screens on the PDA version of the service to place what in industry parlance are called "contextually aware" messages based on a user's specific request for information, as well as their exact location. Want to know where the nearest bar is? Absolut Vodka is happy to give you directions from your location. Want to know what movies are playing? *Batman Begins* is ready to point you to the nearest cineplex.

This kind of relevant targeting is virtually unavailable in any other medium. In the United Kingdom, Kit-Kat worked with mobile marketing firm Enpocket to send SMS messages to office-bound professionals at 4 P.M. in the afternoon—that sweet spot between lunch and dinner. A silly joke was followed with a simple message: "Isn't it time for a Kit-Kat break?"

And Nike, in an effort to promote a free youth football tournament at London's Millennium Dome, was able to target messaging to young male football fans living in London during the half time of the Champions League Semifinal football match.

"This is the one medium you carry with you," says Enpocket CEO Jonathan Linner. "Mobile is the way to reach people at the right place at the right time."

Instead of reaching its target consumer via a cell phone, Coca-Cola recently sent the cell phone to the customer—in the form of a soda can. As part of its "Unexpected Summer" promotion, high-tech soda cans in specially marked Coca-Cola multipacks contained the electronic guts of a combination cell phone and GPS tracker.

By weight and feel, it was just like any other can of Coke. But it looked quite different: The outside of the can featured an activation button, a microphone, and a miniature speaker. When the consumer hit the button, the phone called a special hotline where winners could find out what they'd won—prizes included vacation packages and a 2005 Chevy Equinox sport utility vehicle—and the GPS system remained activated until one of five "national search teams" could locate each winner. See Figure 1-4.

mBranding can also enable consumers to personalize their mobile experience.

Teenyboppers have long pimped out their cell phones with snazzy faceplates, on-screen graphics, and other accoutrements, a notion that's far less interesting, demonstrative, or personal on PCs or other devices. And most analysts agree that such features represent substantial opportunities for building brand affinity and even sales. Look at ringtones. In recent years, over 45 million U.S. consumers have spent $250 million on downloads that enable their phones to chirp out a peppy (some might say irksome) digital rendition of, say, the Loony Tunes anthem or Hoobastank's "Out of Control," for all within earshot of an incoming call.[7, 8] Soon, "ringbacks" (which entertain your callers before you answer the phone) and even full music downloads will further personalize the experience.

Figure 1-4. Not your average can of Coke: This can contained an integrated cell phone and GPS tracker as part of Coca-Cola's Unexpected Summer promotion.

"The mobile phone allows someone to get something on the fly, over the air, 24/7, wherever they are, whenever they want it," says Ralph Simon, an entrepreneur who sold his stake in mobile entertainment firm Moviso to Vivendi Universal, and is now working with music artists such as U2, Justin Timberlake, and the Red Hot Chili Peppers to develop mobile marketing strategies. "Mobile entertainment, and particularly mobile music, tends to be used as a personality badge and acts as a social lubricant."

INTERACTIVITY

The traditional Internet was heralded as the first truly interactive marketing medium, behind, of course, the voice-only telephone. With wireless, these two mediums converge for companies looking to extend the brand experience in a very dynamic way.

The prime example, of course, has long been Fox-TV's *American Idol*. Fans of the popular talent contest can receive alerts, insider news, trivia, behind-the-scenes gossip, and interactive polls on the show's pop-star neophytes and its rancorous panel of judges, which includes 1980s dance diva Paula Abdul and sardonic British import Simon Cowell.

"The show itself is based on viewer participation, and this is just one way to increase that interactivity," says Danielle Perry, a spokesperson for AT&T Wireless, which has since been acquired by Cingular. "'Who got kicked off this week's show?' It reminds me of the old watercooler talk—without the watercooler."[9]

Fans actively place votes, play trivia, enter sweepstakes, make song dedications, and send fan mail to the show's celebrities-in-the-making, from Fantasia Barrino to Clay Aiken to Kelly Clarkson and beyond.

"Anyone can look at the 100 million handsets in users' hands and think to themselves, 'I'd love to build a relationship with that person,'" says Lucy Hood, senior vice president of content for Fox's parent company, News Corporation. "We're trying to deepen viewers' relationship with the *American Idol* brand."[10]

And *American Idol* is not alone. TLC's recent miniseries *Trading Spaces: Home Free* was a reality-based home-design-cum-game show that pitted neighbor against neighbor in various design challenges for the chance to have their mortgages paid off. Each week, viewers could vote online, using e-mail or text messaging, for the contestants they'd like to see advance to the next round. During one promotion for the show, viewers who sent in their e-mail addresses via cell phones were entered into a sweepstakes for the chance to have their own mortgages paid off. "We had tens of thousands of viewers submit their e-mail," says Craig Shapiro, vice president of wireless services for mobile entertainment and marketing firm Proteus. After each Sunday's show, viewers received text messages to ask them to vote online for the contestants they thought did the best job on the previous night's show. They then received subsequent reminders and news items throughout the week.

"Suddenly, this week's show is over, but you're still interacting with the *Trading Spaces* brand," says Shapiro.

Clear Channel has explored other forms of mobile interactivity. During a concert featuring Nickelback, Kid Rock, and Ludicris at the Red Rocks Amphitheater near Denver, audience members could participate in polls and band trivia, as well as send text and picture messages, via a Jumbotron screen on stage for all to see.

Just about any company, in any category, can appreciate the two-way nature of wireless.

In Japan, for instance, Lipton's worked with DoCoMo's i-mode service and interactive ad firm OgilvyOne to develop a Web site called Re-Fresh! to promote the company's ready-to-drink tea beverage. The site featured content about how tea enhances people's moods. Users, the majority of whom accessed the site via their mobile phones, were able to take a personality test and do a mood check. And those who opted to receive messages were sent fun-filled e-mails daily to provide little pick-me-ups along the lines of the brand's personality.[11]

"By communicating with consumers through the mobile phone, you can deliver your message right to their hip pocket," says Wes Bray, founder of mobile marketing firm Hip Cricket. "Consumers leave the house every morning, and they bring their keys, their wallet, their purse, and their cell phones. This is a unique medium in the sense that you can interact with them on a direct, one-on-one basis."

There's no reason that this kind of interaction couldn't be used to enhance the in-store experience as well. The ability to gather feedback and customer input when it's most top-of-mind—as opposed to hoping a customer will mail in a survey or remember to send an e-mail—could prove immensely valuable to certain retailers. Surveys available on a wireless Web site, and advertised in-store, for instance, could create a powerful touch point, and possibly open the way for creating an ongoing dialogue with consumers.

MOBILITY

Wireless is also about taking your favorite services and applications with you. Case in point: E*TRADE, Schwab, Fidelity, Harrisdirect, and other financial institutions have all deployed "mBanking" services to offer customers real-time stock quotes, news, and wireless trading via Web-enabled cell phones, PDAs, and pagers. Today, about 25,000 customers currently use Schwab Wireless, where they monitor indexes, place trades, and manage their accounts via wireless devices. And demand is expected to explode over the next decade.[12]

Jupiter Research predicts that while most online trades initiated by consumers will continue to be made through their desktop PCs, a growing percentage of wireless trading will be composed of responses to brokers' recommendations sent via SMS and e-mail.[13]

In this scenario, clients receive secure messages with options to make a specified trade, edit it, reject it, or request a representative to follow up e-mail notification of a trade with a phone call.

Such "responsive" trading already accounts for upward of 17.6 percent of all online trade commissions, and could soon top $1 billion in commission revenues, according to Jupiter. No doubt other such service extensions will arise to capitalize on this level of connectivity in a variety of industry segments, from travel and hospitality to manufacturing and media.

In addition to the obvious ability to place a cell phone call, AOL Moviefone, MovieTickets.com, and Ticketmaster all offer wireless Internet services that let you find the nearest movie theatre, check movie listings, and in some cases, purchase tickets while on the go.

Even eBay has gone wireless. Pocket Auctions for eBay enables subscribers to several wireless carriers to access popular eBay features from their mobile phones. They can conduct searches, place bids, view pictures, and check their personalized My eBay auction-monitoring pages, where they can track up to thirty eBay auctions at a time.

"Pocket Auctions for eBay also alerts the user through their phone when they've been outbid or when an auction has ended, enabling users to respond immediately to real-time events," says Alex Poon, cofounder of Bonfire Media, the mobile services firm the auction giant teamed up with to deliver the service.[14]

Other companies are simply extending the brand experience to folks on the go. *The Princeton Review* has experimented with a new service called "Prep for the SAT," which sends SAT practice questions to cell phones. After each drill, scores can be sent to parents via e-mail or SMS. Likewise, the *New York Times* offers news digests to consumers via several wireless carriers. And its popular crossword puzzle is available to Verizon Wireless subscribers. Game play includes a sophisticated user interface that features a zoom mode for a close-up view, and auto-expanding, scrollable clue boxes for fast viewing. Users can navigate their crossword puzzle clue-by-clue or cell-by-cell.

"[Wireless] extends our brand into a new, and pretty interesting, consumer area," says Martin Nisenholtz, chief executive officer of New York Times Digital. According to Nisenholtz, the handheld experience is just the beginning. "As the PC has become increasingly untethered, and as Wi-Fi becomes more and more popular as a distribution channel, we'll be part of that simply because we're part of the PC [based Internet experience]."

That's true for just about every online retailer.

"Jeff Bezos estimates by the year 2010, 100 percent of Amazon transactions will happen wirelessly," says business futurist Jaclyn Easton, author of *Going Wireless*. "You might think, 'Wait a second, I'm not going to buy every book or CD off of my [PDA].' And you're right, you probably won't. But you will probably be doing it off of your wireless local area network at home, or your laptop when you're sitting in an airport lounge waiting to board a flight."[15]

As we'll see in Chapter Three, when it comes to the power of wireless interactivity, nothing compares to games. With titles like *Splinter Cell: Pandora Tomorrow*, and *Final Fantasy IV*, it's easy to see that a whole new world of mobile experiences built around popular branded properties is, quite literally, at hand.

IMMERSION

Consumer devices aside, wireless offers companies the ability to create competitive advantage independent of cell phones, MP3 players, or PCs.

Among the most notable examples is red-hot fashion retailer Prada's "Epicenter" stores in New York and Los Angeles. As a shopper picks up a $2,500 dark gray suit or a $700 black leather shoulder bag, specially designed displays read RFID "smart tags" on the items, and then project video clips of runway models and information about availability, cut, color options, and more on nearby displays. Clerks use Wi-Fi–enabled tablet PCs to check inventories or access client histories. And when the shopper takes garments into dressing rooms, scanners read the tags and information about the item, and possible accessories are displayed on a nearby touch screen.

No slacker itself, Wal-Mart has required 200 of its top suppliers to use RFID tags on pallets of products so the retailer can streamline its already legendary supply chain to keep down costs to consumers. One day, the same technology will be used on store shelves, where monitors will alert store clerks when supplies run low of everything from root beer to Rice Krispies.

At this writing, a single RFID tag costs anywhere from $.20

to $100, depending on its capabilities. But as prices become more affordable, the technology could be used to bring intelligence to everyday grocery items. The outcome may one day include consumer product innovations such as clothes that conduct transactions without shoppers ever waiting in line and frozen dinners that transmit cooking instructions to microwave ovens.

"I'll tell you why it will happen: because it improves the customer's experience," says Easton. "It's worth it to ConAgra, which makes most of our frozen food. When someone says that, with an RFID tag that communicates with the microwave oven, my food will be perfectly cooked, for the five cents it would add to the cost of the dinner, it's worth it."[16]

Even household appliances are being imbued with this transparent, or "invisible," wireless connectivity. Whirlpool, Sunbeam, and other appliance manufactures have reportedly been developing "smart appliances" that periodically transmit diagnostic reports so the company, or the retailer that sold the appliance, can stay on top of maintenance and even download new software enhancements wirelessly.

GETTING *THERE*

All of this is just the beginning.

As you're about to see, many other present-day initiatives put the advantages of mBranding to good use—in advertising, in m-commerce, in intelligent places and retail environments, and in sales and service and more.

Of course, whether these and other developments collectively help create a society that evolves to resemble the world of *There* is anyone's guess. But one thing is clear: Something cool—and very important—is happening on the wireless frontier. And in the decade ahead, it's going to change expectations for consumers—and the companies that serve them—in ways most of us can't even yet imagine.

Don Peppers:
1:1 Marketing Goes Wireless

As an influential thought-leader whose groundbreaking books include *Enterprise One-to-One: Tools for Competing in the Interactive Age* and *Return on Customer: The Revolutionary New Way to Maximize the Value of Your Customers*, Peppers advises a Who's Who of international marketers—AT&T, Ford, and 3M, among others—who count on him for insight on using technology to build unbreakable customer loyalty.

But that proposition is about to become increasingly complex, he says, as the convergence of wireless technologies and global positioning systems transforms the notion of reaching customers where they live.

RICK MATHIESON: How will mobility change our idea of what constitutes the "brand experience?"

DON PEPPERS: The most compelling aspect of mobility is the continuous management of evolving relationships with individual consumers. You can be continuously connected with a customer, not just when he's sitting in front of a computer. You can actually get feedback, and real transactions, on a real-time basis—it's as if you're tethered to your customer's life. And that means there is tremendous opportunity in using mobility to increase the value of each customer, and your value to him or her.

Today, most of us can barely imagine life without a cell phone. Consumers are getting used to always-on communications, and those communications are gaining utility. As a result, companies that provide services and maintain relationships with customers are going to have to participate in this channel. And yet, companies are going to have to do it in a way that is nonintrusive, because nothing will give a customer a bigger red face with respect to a company than if that company begins to interrupt him or her in order to try to sell them stuff.

Martha [Rogers, my coauthor] and I have a new concept in *Return on Customer*. Our argument is that for a company, it's the customers that create all value. And like any asset, customers ought to be evaluated for what kind of return we get on them. Our central mission becomes finding ways to increase short-term profits, while promoting behavior that increases the long-term value of that customer. And usually, that can only happen when we help customers understand how to get the most value out of us. It happens when we earn the customer's trust, treat the customer the way they'd like to be treated, and actually act in their best interests in a way that's mutually beneficial.

For instance, if I'm Ameritrade, and I have a customer who trades three or four times a day when he's in his office, but he doesn't trade when he's traveling, I'd strongly consider giving him a BlackBerry and a wireless trading account. It's a win/win for both of us. The customer gets convenience, and the company gains potential new revenues.

There's also a role for mobility in connecting the mobile salesperson and delivery person with the mother ship, so to speak. Whether we're talking about the phone repairman who has access to his customer's records, or the delivery driver who reconfigures the product on the fly based on initial customer feedback, mobility has a great deal to do with the intimacy with which any business can serve its customers.

RM: Many think mobility will enable further disintermediation of services. But you envision the rise of "Data Aggregation Agents" that enable companies to deliver 1:1 services based on my needs and location—as long as they play by my rules. What's the business model for these DAAs?

DP: Instead of giving out personal information to every vendor that I might deal with in the mobile medium—my news service, my broker, my concierge, my travel agent—I'm going to want one entity that remembers my preferences and needs, but that provides me anonymity.

One entity that knows my account numbers for all the different companies I deal with, across a lot of different platforms and different mobile media. And that entity is something we call the "Data Aggregation Agent."

The DAA is going to simplify the consumer's life because it will save them a great deal of time and energy. I'm not going to want to fill in my speed dial numbers, my friends' names and e-mail addresses, my credit card numbers, my social security numbers, my everything, for everybody. The DAA will store all that information for me in one place, and then partition out data to companies as I see fit. It's just a hypothetical, science fiction possibility, of course. But I think it's a compelling new business model for the future, and could have a tremendous impact on the nature of competition in this medium.

RM: You're talking about some pretty valuable information. Seems like a lot of companies would fight over playing the role of DAA.

DP: You bet they will. Already, there are a lot of infantile battles going on among businesses that all think that they can be Data Aggregation Agents. A very simple example was when Boeing started selling airlines on the idea of connecting airplanes to the Internet. Are you surprised by the fact that American Airlines doesn't want its high-value business passengers dialing up on the Internet and connecting suddenly to the Boeing Web site?

The same exact battle is going to play out in telematics on the road. We've met with companies in the automotive manufacturing space, as well as companies in the mobile communications electronics space, and they have the same basic designs on the customer: I want that customer to be my customer.

But in the end, everybody can't win. The most compelling business model is one where the consumer gets the value. And the value I'm getting if I'm a consumer is convenience, relevance, and not having to fill out the same form or keep track of different account numbers. So there are a lot of reasons why the Data Aggregation Agent model is going to work. And that role could be filled by a wireless carrier like Verizon. It could be filled by an airline. It could be AOL or Yahoo. Or it could be filled by completely new players.

RM: As wireless moves into the in-store experience, what opportunities will there be to maximize the experience for customers?

DP: I think RFID technology, in particular, has a great deal of potential for that. The science fiction future of RFID is that I have my credit card in my wallet, I walk into the grocery store, I put a bunch of shopping products in my bags and I walk out the door and take them home, and I'm automatically billed for them. I don't need to stop at the checkout counter, and I don't have to do anything but walk out with my products. I think that will be highly desirable for consumers. But there is a big-brother aspect to the technology that is awakening some of the Luddites in the business, who say, gee, I don't know if I want companies tracking every movement that I make, and so forth. But I think on balance, consumer convenience is going to be the trump card. That said, whether it's in-store, or out in the world via consumer cell phones, companies will have to be very careful about how they apply wireless technologies.

In this medium, you're playing with fire when it comes to privacy. It's impossible to architect the regulatory structure in such a way to ensure that you're not going to get hit with some kind of privacy problem.

The best defense is to adopt a holistic view of your business. In my conception, every business would visualize their service in terms of treating their customers the way you'd want to be treated. The golden rule of marketing, if you will. With that in mind, you simply can't go wrong.

RM: The same applies to 1:1 mobile advertising, no doubt.

DP: If you're driving down the street and an ad comes on because you're a block away from McDonald's, you're going to be extremely irritated. And if you have to listen to an ad before you place a call, you're going to be pissed.

But unlike a lot of folks, I don't think that means push is going to always be excluded from people's requirements—as long as it's pushed at the customer's initiation and doesn't trespass on the legitimate use of their time.

For instance, if I execute a trade on my cell phone, and you're my online brokerage, I don't mind you piggybacking an ad for an offer I might be interested in at the bottom of an order confirmation. Or if you're Amazon, you might recommend an additional book based on my profile. Or American Airlines might send an e-mail about cheap tickets I can buy because they haven't sold enough seats to the locations on my preferred destination list.

I can see a lot of potential for that kind of push message—as long as the customer says it's okay to send them. Because whether we're talking about an ad message, a service, or a transaction, it's all about using mobile technologies to add value to our customers' lives based on what they want, where—and when—they want it.

If you get it right, you win big. If you get it wrong, you're history.

CHAPTER TWO

Reach Out & Sell Someone

The Top 10 Secrets of
Successful Mobile Advertising

Like no day before it, wireless advertising went legit the day the Material Girl went mobile. A master marketer with a penchant for streetwise reinvention, Madonna was among the first global brand names to make advertising campaigns delivered to consumers' cell phones seem downright dope. Not just to consumers in Asia and Europe, who'd long been exposed to mobile marketing from the likes of Procter & Gamble and Unilever, but to wireless newbies who just happen to be the ultimate arbiters of pop culture cool: America's teenagers.

In the run-up to the release of Madonna's hit singles, "American Life" and "Hollywood," Warner Records worked with mobile marketing firm ipsh! to enlist the songstress's most cutting-edge fans to build some serious buzz using nothing more than their Web-enabled cell phones.

Here's how it worked. A banner ad on the Madonna.com Web site enabled fans to enter in any U.S. cell phone number and send a text message to themselves and a friend. Once they received the text message, recipients were prompted to dial in a secret phone number to hear clips of the singles and learn how to download the entire songs before they hit stores and the Internet. See Figure 2-1.

Figure 2-1. Madonna's use of mobile marketing sparked a revolution of wireless ad campaigns in the United States. Image: ipsh!

"The idea was to create a Web interface that made it easy for users to send a text message that would essentially deliver the track directly to their cell phone, and their friends' cell phones," says ipsh! CEO Nihal Mehta, whose San Francisco–based firm has gone on to produce numerous mobile advertising campaigns for pop stars Usher, Lil' Romeo, and Godsmack.

According to Mehta, the Madonna campaign cost less than $20,000. Over a one-month period, fans sent 30,000 of the special text messages. And 62.1 percent of recipients dialed in to hear the songs—generating fan enthusiasm that contributed to over 650,000 sales of the *American Life* album—and further cementing Madonna's reputation for innovation and staying power.

"TREADING LIGHTLY"

That was way back in 2003. Today, Madonna runs her own mobile Web site, which beckons fans to "reinvent your phone," and "get into the groove" with Madonna ringtones, graphic background "wallpaper," and other items that are purchasable directly from mobile handsets. Inspired by Madonna's foray into the medium, as well as a burgeoning number of other such success stories, today's most innovative marketers have literally flocked to the wireless world.

Spending on wireless advertising already approaches nearly $1 billion annually—and could top $5 billion by 2007, according to the Mobile Marketing Association, an industry trade group based in Mountain View, California.[1] But today, many marketers are still struggling to find ways to deliver their messages via the small screens of mobile devices without ticking consumers off.

After all, Madonna's success notwithstanding, the idea of sending advertising messages to consumers' cell phones and PDAs does seem risible, at best. The screens are too small. The intrusion, too offensive. The experience, too limited. With consumers footing the bill for the connection, the proposition seems downright wack.

"Advertisers are going to go where the customer is," says Carrie Himelfarb, vice president of sales for New York City–based Vindigo Studios, which produces the Vindigo family of mobile services. "[But] we're treading very lightly with the ad model on phones. Consumers pay for the airtime, and we don't want to freak them out."

To that end, a number of wireless technology and service providers, marketers, and advertising agencies have been spanning the globe throughout the first half of this decade, conducting market trials on the efficacy of wireless advertising.

What's emerging is a glimpse at what's working, what's not, what's coming, and what principles will prove most profitable over the near term.

#1: SIZE MATTERS

The typical display screens on mobile devices are still quite small, occasionally still monochromatic, and, in some cases, text-only— hardly the ideal venue for delivering compelling advertising.

As a result, text-based SMS has proven the most popular advertising format so far. And no wonder: SMS costs just pennies to send, and the results can be phenomenal. Tests in Japan by interactive advertising firm DoubleClick, for instance, showed that such text ads pull an amazing 14 percent response rate.[2] Not bad, when you consider SMS messages are text only and can be no longer than 160 characters, including spaces and punctuation. By comparison, the average click-through rate of the standard, fully animated Internet ad banner has held steady for some time at an uninspiring one-half of 1 percent.[3]

"The key is tying these short messages to information the user has requested," says Himelfarb. A Vindigo campaign for Perrier, conducted during fashion week in New York City, promoted the froufrou bottled water brand as well as a special Fashion Week VIP Sweepstakes. When a Vindigo user searched for restaurants, bars, or cultural events in their immediate vicinity, they got a message from Perrier. Over 8 percent of recipients subsequently opted to have product and sweepstakes information sent to their e-mail addresses.

Not surprisingly, says Himelfarb, the advertising professionals who tend to "get" SMS marketing typically hail from outdoor advertising—billboards and other signage—where space is at a premium, and copy must carry massive punch with a minimal number of words.

Jonathan Linner, CEO of mobile marketing firm Enpocket, agrees. "If you're going to make something interesting and funny, include a call to action, and get your message across very quickly, you've got to be really talented creatively," he says.

Case in point: Murphy's stout beer. In an effort to add personality to the brand and strengthen its relationship with consumers, Murphy's launched the "Murphy's Challenge" campaign, where consumers were sent unfinished limericks via SMS and asked to send back a creative solution. See Figure 2-2.

The same systems that enable SMS also enable short codes— those typically four- to five-digit numbers that can be used to respond to special offers. Increasingly, short codes are popping up on product packaging and in print and broadcast advertising.

Cereal giant Kellogg's, for instance, placed short codes on 80 million cereal and snack boxes to tie in with sweepstakes and game promotions. Cell phone users could send the word "WIN" to a four-digit short code, where they could participate in a sweepstakes; or "PLAY" to another short code, where they could participate in trivia based on popular television shows on Cartoon Network. Sweepstakes winners received a Mazda MPV Minivan customized to resemble the Scooby Doo Mystery Machine. See Figure 2-3.

"As a direct response medium, mobile is very convincing for brands, because they get direct tracking of how many interactions they're facilitating," says Carsten Boers, CEO of U.K.–based mobile

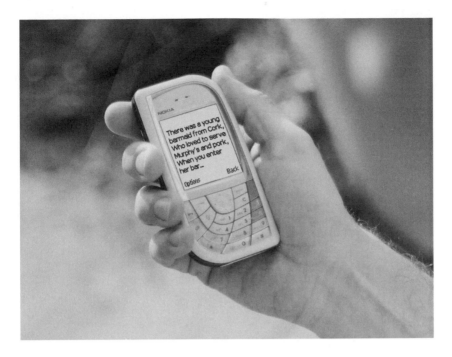

Figure 2-2. This creative SMS campaign for Murphy's brought flair to this traditional beverage maker brand. Photo: Enpocket.

marketing firm Flytxt. "Obviously, from a branding perspective, it's great to have a dialogue, rather than just a broadcast."

And it's beginning to catch on. According to research from Enpocket, 2 percent of U.S. cell phone users have sent text messages to a number on product packaging, 1.3 percent to an advertisement, 1.6 percent to a TV show, 1.1 percent to a magazine, and .7 percent to a radio show.[4]

In other scenarios, even packaged food in grocery stores can include short codes that consumers can enter to receive coupons that they can redeem at the cash register.

"If you're really looking for a depth of interaction—that moment of truth—a very meaningful way to interact is to provide a menu planner," says John Ricketts of Ogilvy Asia/Pacific. Ricketts says short codes on packaged food can lead to wireless Web sites or text messages that provide menus for planning a meal around that product.

"Banner" style advertising on the slightly larger screens of

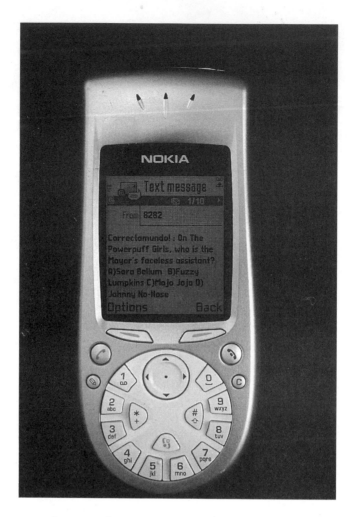

Figure 2-3. Kellogg's and Cartoon Network reached out to wireless consumers with an SMS trivia campaign designed to inject some cool into both brands.

PDAs is another option for mobile marketers, with a cost per thousand ad impressions of $1 to $35, depending on the service. But today, more people gravitate to cell phones versus PDAs; in the United States, there are over 180 million cell phone users, and only about 1.4 million PDA users.[5] As a result, it's the phone that's emerging as the platform of choice for consumers and, by extension, mobile marketers.

On both platforms, an increasing number of response models are emerging, including:

▶ Clickable coupons that can be redeemed for product discounts at retail stores by showing the onscreen coupon to a store clerk or by enabling clerks to scan an onscreen bar code directly into the store's POS system

▶ "Click-to-e-mail," which instructs the advertiser to send more information to a previously supplied e-mail address

▶ "Tap-through screens" that link consumers to more information on a promotion

▶ A prompt to initiate a cell phone call to a ticket office or call center—referred to as a "call-through" in industry parlance

Increasingly, new multimedia message service (MMS)–based advertising delivers pictures and even full video and audio, for a more television-like experience, as are actual mobile Web sites, or sites designed to be accessed through wireless devices.

In the United Kingdom, Warner Brothers and Enpocket have been using MMS to send full-motion movie trailers to consumers who opt-in to receive them. And threeoclock.com provides consumers with free access to full-color magazines—and their associated advertising messages—via cell phones.

Without a doubt, MMS will literally transform the wireless experience, and will become increasingly important to marketers as carriers work out standards for delivering such capabilities across various devices and networks. For now, however, the most prevalent model in these early days is a kind of reverse-MMS—getting consumers to send MMS to the brand.

New York City–based *Jane* magazine, for instance, conducted an experiment using MMS to connect advertisers and consumers in the mobile medium. The promotion, dubbed "Jane Talks Back," urged readers to "Grab your camera phone and take a picture of any and all ads in this magazine." When they did, readers received freebies, sweepstakes, MP3s, and *Jane*-related information. See Figure 2-4.

Why this approach? Eva Dillon, vice president and publisher of *Jane*, told the *New York Times* that readers "use picture and texting functions on their cell phones almost more frequently than they talk . . . We were brainstorming what we could do that would make

Figure 2-4. Jane readers used camera phones to snap pictures of print ads as part of an MMS promotion.

them get involved in our programs in a way that's fun and speaks to them—in a way that they speak to each other."[6]

#2: NO PUSHING ALLOWED

One of the biggest misconceptions about wireless is the idea that we'll one day walk down the street and be bombarded with digital coupons for a cup of coffee at the nearest Starbucks, a sweater at Bloomies, or a burger at McDonald's. That sort of practice is called "push advertising." In the early part of this decade, it seemed everyone talked about this form of location-based advertising—call it the Latte Scenario—based on your physical whereabouts.

Forget about it. We'd never put up with that kind of spam or the invasion of privacy. The immediacy of the wireless medium is much more powerful—and less invasive—than that. When it comes to wireless advertising, SMS or otherwise, most experts agree that communication must be driven by the consumer responding to a promotion or on an opt-in basis. This "pull" model is expected to be the preferred format for most, if not all, mobile marketing.

"What will happen is, instead of you being bombarded by messages on your GPS–sensitive mobile phone as you walk by a Starbucks, you will be sending a message to Starbucks, asking, 'Do you carry mints?' or, 'Is there a special for a loyal Starbucks customer?' and then you'll receive the offers," says trend-spotter Michael Tchong, a columnist for *Fast Company* and founder of Trendscape, a San Francisco–based media firm.

Those who share Tchong's view had better be right. According to reports in the *Wall Street Journal*, only a tiny percentage of cell phone subscribers say they're receptive to mobile advertising. Citing a study of 5,510 U.S. cell phone users from research firm Yankee Group, the *Journal* says only 20 percent reported they'd been the recipient of a text ad. Of that group, 9 percent said it bothered them, while another 9 percent deleted it. Only 2 percent said they received an ad that was relevant to them.[7]

The risk, of course, is in the consumer outrage that resulted in the U.S. National Do Not Call List, which forbids telemarketers from calling specially registered consumers.

"We're talking about very personal devices," says Lauren Bigaleow, an industry expert who conducted a number of early research studies on mobile marketing. "It's really important for users to ask to receive information, not just receive it."[8]

Indeed, while consumer dissonance over spam has restrained Internet and even some mobile marketing in the United States, Europe's Privacy and Electronic Communications Directive makes it absolutely illegal to send mobile promotions to consumers without their explicit permission.

By requiring opt-in participation, such actions have helped legitimize European mobile advertising as a viable channel for brands consumers know and trust.

Many hope the United States will follow suit, citing the federal CAN Spam Act as a step in the right direction—even if most view it as unenforceable. The law levies a fine of $250 for each unsolicited e-mail pitch, up to $6 million for serious offenders.[9]

Of course, just as fast as laws can be enacted to protect consumers, illegitimate marketers find ways to circumvent them. Since the CAN Spam Act went into effect, unsolicited junk email has actually increased to 80 percent of all e-mail sent, up from 60 percent before the law was enacted.[10] Unfortunately, spammers are finding fertile ground in other emerging media. Over 500 million "spim" messages (spam sent over an Instant Messaging system) were sent in 2003.[11] And over 1.2 billion SMS–based spam messages are sent a year to mobile subscribers worldwide.[12] In fact, in Japan, where SMS is more popular than e-mail, DoCoMo blocks over 960 million spam messages each day—more than 80 percent of all incoming SMS messages—from reaching 46 million subscribers.[13]

To head off the problem, many early mobile marketers are being extremely—some even might say egregiously—careful. Case in point: As first reported by *ADWEEK*, in order to receive movie updates, trivia, SMS polls, games, and ringtones related to the release of *Harry Potter and the Prisoner of Azkaban*, fans had to fill out a form at the movie's Web site, which states in no uncertain terms that recipients may be charged their cell phone company's regular airtime charges for messages sent to their handsets.[14] Once the form was sent, recipients received a confirmation number on their phones that they then had to register on the Web site before they would begin receiving content—called a "confirmed opt-in," according to the Mobile Marketing Association.

With that kind of rigorous vetting, you can rest assured participants really, really want Harry, Hermione, and Sirius Black to be part of their mobile experience. Then again, given the title of the movie, there's extra incentive to keep the mobile promotion as irony-free as possible. See Figure 2-5.

To help head off the problem, the Mobile Marketing Association is working on promoting a code of ethics for its members. Key among its principles: consumer choice and control. With a jaw-dropping 25 to 30 percent churn rate, the wireless carriers also have a vested interest in keeping consumers' cool while opening up the airwaves to marketers.

When done right, permission-based, opt-in scenarios can pay big dividends.

The History Channel, for instance, teamed up with Enpocket to send 100,000 text messages promoting its upcoming *Barbarians*

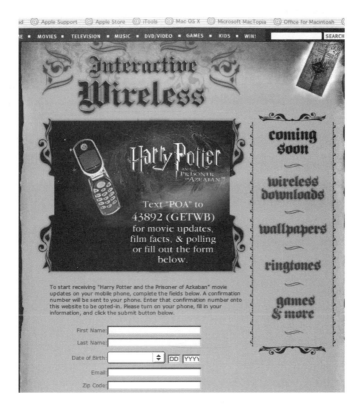

Figure 2-5. Marketers for Harry Potter made absolutely sure mobile consumers—many of them kids—were absolutely, positively clear about what they were signing up for.

television show to viewers who'd opted to receive such messages. Three days after the program aired, a survey of 200 people who received the message found that 88 percent read the message, 18 percent watched the *Barbarians* program, and 12 percent forwarded the message to a friend.

The network followed up with mobile promotions for *Decisive Battles* and *Command Decisions*, in which viewers could enter 8288 on their cell phones to interact in real time with the show—answering questions on famous battles, from the Greek wars to the Gulf War, via SMS. Contestants were entered into a sweepstakes to win one of fifty copies of *Rome: Total War*, a 3-D video game, or the grand prize—a Panasonic home digital entertainment center.

#3: INTEGRATION IS THE NAME OF THE GAME

Most experts agree that wireless advertising works best as part of an integrated multimedia campaign that includes any combination of print, outdoor, or broadcast advertising.

A two-month SMS–based advertising campaign in Italy, for instance, resulted in a 9 percent increase in sales for Dunkin' Donuts stores in Rome.

The interactive promotion, designed to increase sales at seven retail locations, enabled consumers to respond to print, outdoor, and broadcast advertisements by entering five-digit short codes into their Web-enabled mobile phones.

In return, they received a downloadable coupon for a free cup of coffee with the purchase of one of the donut giant's fifty-two variations of pastries—from the Apple Crumb Cake Donut to its worldwide favorite, the Boston Krème Donut. Once in stores, consumers could enter a drawing for a free Piaggio motorbike.

"Young people between eighteen and thirty are the largest users of SMS in Italy, and are also a target market for Dunkin' Donuts," says Michael Correletti, international business manager for Dunkin' Donuts's worldwide franchise network. "This was an opportunity to communicate directly to core customers."[15]

The eight-week campaign, created in conjunction with wireless logistics provider Mobileway, featured promotional codes for print, broadcast, and poster advertisements, so response rates could be tracked by medium.

During its first three weeks, the campaign resulted in a 20 percent increase in overall sales, with 9 percent directly traceable to the SMS component of the campaign.

About 82 percent of all SMS senders came into a store, usually within one day. The value of the coupon was more than it costs to send an SMS, so the result was a fun and effective promotion that provided real value to all parties.

The Dunkin' Donuts initiative points to the power of using SMS as an interactive element in a broader, multimedia campaign: Nearly 30 percent of respondents downloaded the coupon after hearing radio commercials, for instance.

More important, the initiative underscores the growing interest in SMS as a marketing channel to three-quarters of the 280 million European mobile phone owners who use SMS to communicate with friends, family, and business colleagues.[16, 17]

In fact, in some parts of Europe, SMS usage exceeds that of the wireline Internet. In one study from Forrester Research, SMS–based marketing attracted an average response rate of 11 percent—or seven times that of European print-based direct mail.

No wonder a survey of 205 direct marketers by the Federation of European Direct Marketing and Forrester Research revealed that 21 percent of respondents already use SMS marketing at least occasionally, and 12 percent have at least tried it.[18] Many U.S. marketers are also looking into SMS as a marketing channel.

"Mobile is just one touchpoint in an integrated campaign," says Barry Peters, vice president of relationship marketing and evolving media for Carat Interactive. "Large brands should not do mobile marketing just for the sake of mobile marketing. They should work with their agencies to understand the opportunities, and whether this makes sense as part of the marketing mix."

Many are doing just that: Stealing a page from Yahoo's playbook, brand giant Unilever created an interactive Times Square billboard for its Dove-brand beauty soap. Tied to a print and broadcast campaign of the same theme, the billboard flashed a series of women's faces and asked, "What is beautiful?" Pedestrians could place votes on which images they found most beautiful, and tallies were displayed in real time.[19] As part of an integrated television, print, and online campaign for Herbal Essences Highlights, Procter & Gamble created a promotion in which consumers who sent a text message to "Dare to Streak" got a chance to be invited to the "Ultimate Streaking Party" at the House of Blues at Mandalay Bay in Las Vegas.

Meanwhile, Hershey's Chocolate Milk posted short codes on point-of-purchase displays and packaging based on an X-Games promotion. Consumers could enter the "cap code" printed on bottle caps for the chance to win a trip for ten to the popular extreme sporting event. See Figure 2-6.

And MTV's "Choose or Lose" campaign teamed up with the

Figure 2-6. More and more advertisers use short codes as a way for consumers to interact with brands.

Federal Election Commission to enable cell phone users to participate in polls about political issues leading up to the 2004 presidential
elections, and to take part in a mock vote via text messaging.

Heck, even the Pope has gone mobile. Cell phone subscribers in
the United States and Europe can subscribe to the Vatican's wireless

service, called "The Pope's Thought of the Day," to receive homilies, prayers, and guidance from the Pontiff's teachings.

Still, everyone should take heed: SMS's sky-high response rates won't last forever. SMS is still the purview of early adopters, and the novelty factor will no doubt wear off.

Likewise, advertising in the wireless world will change dramatically as new high-bandwidth 3G and, someday, 4G networks deliver a richer wireless experience with TV-like audiovisuals, combined with fully interactive features.

#4: ENTERTAINMENT ROCKS

Many experts agree that the most powerful advertising models are ones that facilitate communication, provide instant gratification, or offer some kind of entertaining diversion. As witnessed above, polling and trivia are extremely popular motifs.

"With the mobile channel, what's working is a lot of interactive messaging around brand promotion that has entertainment value, and provides some benefit to the consumer to participate in that interaction," says Jim Manis of mobile marketing firm m-Qube.

To promote its sponsorship of the 2004 Summer Olympics, McDonald's launched the largest on-packaging, text-messaging promotion in U.S. history. More than 250 million McDonald's to-go bags featured an Olympics-related trivia game targeted exclusively to AT&T Wireless text-messaging users. Consumers could test their Olympic IQ by using the text-messaging feature on their cell phones to answer questions printed on the bags.

Meanwhile, in one of the United Kingdom's largest SMS sweepstakes campaigns yet, Coca-Cola Great Britain launched TXT FOR MUSIC, a promotion that offers consumers the chance to win free music CDs and concert tickets in exchange for using their cell phones to enter short codes printed on over 200 million bottles and cans of Coke and Cherry Coke.

The six-month promotion was supported by a massive radio,

television, magazine, and newspaper campaign that ensured maximum exposure throughout the United Kingdom.

Coca-Cola won't say how much it spent on the campaign. But industry watchers say spending by Coke and partners, which included marketing communications firm bd-ntwk and media giant EMAP, could easily have topped $5 million (U.S.)—making it the largest U.K.–based campaign yet to put SMS center stage.

"[It was] by far the biggest SMS campaign in terms of scale and exposure to consumers," says Lars Becker, founder of Flytxt, which was the agency behind the promotion.[20]

Coke's TXT 2 COLLECT promotion used a credit collection model that enticed consumers to register in an instant-win competition for concerts and other premiums, and then guaranteed that everyone at least won something.

In this case, consumers accumulated credits that could be saved up and exchanged for a choice of eight CD singles and five compilation albums from popular U.K. artists such as Kym Marsh and Busted.

"This moves the [mobile promotion] model toward building loyalty—and an ongoing dialogue—with the youth audience, which can be very hard to reach," says Darren Siddall, a senior analyst for research firm GartnerG2 in London.[21]

Players registered via cell phone, or through the special Coke Web site. Each time they entered a new code, a ring-back feature alerted players to their accumulated points. And players could also check their credits via the Web.

Of course, the more you drank—and the larger the bottle—the more credits you won.

Coca-Cola USA followed suit, enabling consumers to redeem cap codes printed inside of the caps on specially marked 20-ounce bottles of Coke and entering "2653" (COKE) via SMS. Participants accrue points, or "Decibels," in their Decibel Central account at Cokemusic.com, that they can use toward music and other items.

During a study of 1,000 U.S.–based cell phone users, researchers discovered that such entertainment-oriented advertising resulted in a 58 percent ad recall rate after four months—with 15 percent resulting in some action, such as a store visit, and 3 percent resulting in a purchase.[22] See Figure 2-7.

As you've probably noticed by now, the entertainment industry has had a particularly high level of success with these sorts of campaigns. Witness Madonna. Pop star Ashlee Simpson has used similar promotions for her album, *Autobiography*. And even Madonna's spiritual goddaughter, Britney Spears, has used text alerts, personalized voice messages, and location-sensitive text alerts to lead con-

Figure 2-7. "TXT 2 Collect" models driving ongoing interactions between brands and their customers. Photo: Enpocket.

sumers to stores selling her perfume brand, *Curious*. And there are many others.

Premiere magazine, for instance, used wireless to create a fun two-way interaction with the magazine's current readers, as well as introduce the brand to other consumers in a promotion leading up to the Academy Awards.

Print, online, and in-theater advertising asked movie fans to predict the year's award winners by sending a text message using a short code. Participants received a category prediction ballot and breaking movie alerts via their mobile phones. They voted for each award category, one at a time, for a chance to win a trip to Holly-wood, Sony Electronics devices, movie tickets, soundtracks, and other prizes.[23]

"The wireless component is compelling in that it really enriches the experience for [viewers]," says Danielle Perry, spokesperson for AT&T Wireless. "It extends the brand for the entertainment company in a way that's never been done before."[24]

During football's College Bowl season, for instance, ESPN teamed up with Cingular Wireless for the "Cingular Text Challenge," a wireless college football trivia contest. Each week, one lucky fan won a trip for two to the Bowl Championship Series game of their choice. Participants were entered in drawings for hundreds of instant prizes, and a total of thirteen BCS trips were awarded.

Indeed, Cingular has been especially active in mobile promotions. The wireless carrier teamed up with the Yankees Entertainment and Sports Network (YESnetwork) to bring text trivia to New York Yankee baseball fans, for instance. During Yankee pregame shows, announcers presented a Yankees-related question for viewers to vote on from their phone. The votes were tallied in real time, and results were sent to each participant's phone, as well as displayed at the end of the pregame show, and online at YESNetwork .com. Meanwhile, over 14,000 Cingular subscribers took part in an MTV trivia game to win tickets to the MTV Video Music Awards and the chance to win $25,000.

Even blockbuster movies have found ways to capitalize on wireless. For popcorn pictures like *Spiderman 3, Pirates of the Caribbean 2, The Poseidon Adventure*, and others, movie marketers routinely use trivia, polling, screen graphics, movie trailers, and alerts to reach out to consumers through cross-channel, cross-carrier promotional programs using the medium of their choice—SMS, MMS, e-mail, and instant messaging. See Figure 2-8.

"Wireless strengthens the core experience of a movie or TV show by adding a level of interactivity and keeping viewers engaged in a community [of interest]," says Adam Zawel, a Yankee Group analyst who tracks mobile entertainment. "And to the degree to which people use SMS, wireless is a good channel for viral marketing."

Figure 2-8. MMS enables consumers to view movie trailers on their cell phones before they place purchases for tickets. Photo: Enpocket.

#5: SPONSORSHIPS RULE

Harkening back to the golden age of television, sponsorships are expected to be a major model for marketers in every medium in coming years, as consumers continue to tune out advertising, and as brands demand alternative advertising opportunities. The idea: Advertisers sponsor content that may or may not have anything to do with what they sell, but nonetheless targets those who fit their customer profile.

Case in point: Cadillac. The company has launched a "channel" within the Vindigo City Guide that's all about pointing out the trendy night spots, restaurants, and events in a given city. See Figure 2-9.

Figure 2-9. Cadillac Hot Spots leads mobile consumers to all things hip in their immediate vicinity.

"We're building out these extra features that are brought to you by advertisers who want to associate themselves with these consumers, and seem out on the cutting edge," says Himelfarb.

Even decidedly "unsexy" brands are getting into the act. According to reports in the *Wall Street Journal Europe*, Germany-based agrochemicals maker Bayer CropScience, for instance, sends weather alerts by text message to farmers, giving them information on airborne bacteria—as well as related product recommendations.

Sometimes these sorts of sponsored applications come in the form of regularly updated downloads that are cached on the device for access when the user isn't connected to a wireless network. In the United States, for instance, *Maxim* magazine's "Maxim To Go Beer Buddy" serves up news on the latest new beer brands, best picks, expert reviews, bar jokes, and official beer rankings for bar-hoppers everywhere.

In Japan, greeting card giant Hallmark took a different approach. In an effort to launch a mobile greeting card service called Hallmark Hiya, in a market unaccustomed to sending cards for birthdays and anniversaries—much less expressing one's innermost feelings—the company worked with OgilvyOne to create a make-believe soap opera. Consumers could sign up to become part of a "virtual" drama involving seven fictitious friends. Each participant would then periodically receive a message from one of the characters, asking for a response. To do so, the participant would choose from three possible messages, each expressing an intimate feeling or expression. Depending on the selection, the story line would take a different direction, with different dramatic outcomes. At the end of the drama, participants were able to send their own free messages to any one of the seven characters.

Within its first twenty days, over 40,000 consumers signed up to participate in the campaign. Best of all, sales to the Hiya service exceeded a quarter of the company's annual targets within three weeks of launch.[25]

"In Japan, for many parts of the population, mobile really is the dominant medium," says John Ricketts of Ogilvy Asia/Pacific. "In the United States, mobile is still relatively underdeveloped compared to the rest of the world. Here, it's as real as TV being part of your life. It's as real as print media being part of life. It's as real as the Web being part of your life. We haven't been inventing opportunities. The opportunities are coming to us."

#6: IT'S TIME TO GET PERSONAL

Over 90 percent of participants in one IDC study on "consumer tolerance of advertising in emerging media" say they'd be very interested in advertising if it were based on a presubmitted user profile that ensured ads are relevant to them.[26]

Makes sense. There's no use selling Pampers to empty nesters.

But because consumer permission is the golden rule of mobile marketing, advertisers are able to send extremely targeted campaigns based on user demographics and preference. Sometimes that can even mean campaigns within campaigns.

During Coke's TXT 2 COLLECT promotion, for instance, marketers identified consumption patterns among certain segments of its participant base.

"There were certain patrons whose Coke consumption was done ahead of the weekend—moms who were buying household purchases going into the weekend," says Flytxt's Boers. So Coke sent these consumers "double incentives"—double the usual TXT 2 COLLECT points if they bought a 2-liter bottle on the upcoming Friday.

Through similar scenarios, an SMS campaign for Cadbury Schweppes PLC enabled the chocolatier to not only promote its products, but to learn more about consumption habits, such as which types of chocolate are popular in different areas, and at what time of day different people consume different products.

In a promotion aimed at getting seventeen- to thirty-five-year-old women to the movies on Valentine's Day, Orange and Enpocket sent women in this segment a message about going out to see the latest romantic comedy, which they could then forward to their husbands and boyfriends. Forty-one percent of those exposed to the campaign said it influenced them enough to go see the movies.

Mobile marketers typically acquire their consumer lists and profiles in either of two ways:

▶ *Homegrown.* Contest participants are asked to opt-in for future promotions and information, and segmentation is conducted through recorded behavior.

▶ *Farmed-Out.* Carriers can provide lists of consumers who have provided information about themselves and the types of promotions they are amenable to receiving; once the consumer responds to a promotion sent out to that list, the marketer can begin building aggregated profiles.

#7: LOCATION IS (SOMETIMES) WHERE IT'S AT

While some media, such as television, profit from treating consumers as a single mass, the most tantalizing prospect of mobile advertising is the ability to send marketing messages not just to a specific user, but to a specific user in a specific location—the ultimate in contextual messaging.

"The promise of mobile marketing is fulfilling someone's need not just based on time of day, but on where they are," says Himelfarb.

Vindigo's city guide, for instance, serves up ads based on user queries—the nearest Italian restaurant, or a music store within a half-mile radius, for instance—and offers directions, reviews, and special offers based on information users provide.

But Himelfarb is quick to echo others that the much-hyped vision of sending an unsolicited coupon for the nearest Starbucks—the dreaded Latte Scenario—is a dead end.

Instead, it's more typical for consumers to actually enter in their location and tell the service where they're at, launching recommendations based on that supplied location.

In a potentially more compelling option for certain retailers, new Wi-Fi–based Location Enabled Networks (LENs) carve up a wireless network within a store or mall into discrete segments that target users passing through a specified location.

If customers opt in for service, the network can locate them as they pass access points. Such systems can then serve up shopping, dining, or entertainment options to shoppers' cell phones or PDAs based on their location at any specific time. These sorts of experiential branding opportunities can promote specific products or retail establishments on the basis of the customer's predefined preferences and expectations.

NCR Corporation and m-Qube, for instance, are working on solutions to enable retailers and food service operators to increase sales with instant mobile couponing, loyalty, and promotional programs.

In the future, wireless systems will be tied to back-end databases and loyalty programs, says Manis. When you walk into a grocery store, he says, you may enter a code that sends a message to the store's database to let the store know you've arrived, and that you're open to receiving promotions.

So how cool is that? Since you're communicating directly with the store's database, it will keep track of not just what you buy, but what you don't. And the intelligence will be built in to make offers to you based on your personal purchase history.

"If you've been buying beauty products at that store, and then you don't for a while, the assumption is you're buying them somewhere else," says Manis. "So they may push you a coupon—pick up this shampoo for 30 percent off—and you present the coupon at the point of sale as your items are being scanned."

Adding wireless to these existing databases is a fairly easy proposition—and it may finally put all that data collected from supermarket loyalty cards to good use.

"That's the value of mobile," says Manis. "You begin to take advantage of intelligent databases that already exist. And as consumers ask for data, you are actually able to supply it to them, right then and there."

#8: THE MEDIUM IS (STILL) THE MESSAGE

At the Extra Super Store in Rheinberg, Germany, shoppers can wave handheld "shopping assistants" at a video cassette or CD and hear or see clips before making a purchase. And shoppers at twenty-four AltiTunes music stores in the United States carry a PDA–sized device that lets them scan a CD and not only hear selections of music, but also peruse information on band members, album reviews, and discographies.

In the next five years, that functionality will extend to everyone's cell phone and PDA, enabling capabilities that let us scan bar codes to sample music clips before making a purchase, or scan posters, print ads, and retail displays to capture product information wirelessly via the Web. We can already view movie trailers and other media snippets on these small, personal devices. What might be next?

It's important to start exploring the use of other capabilities inherent in the wireless device. For instance, the functionality of many mobile devices to keep schedules and manage personal contacts—addresses, phone numbers, birthdays, and so on—may be waiting for opportunities. Smart marketers will find ways to integrate wirelessly transmitted communications with these built-in capabilities.

If you're a retailer, why not enable me to opt in to a service that sends me gift ideas tagged to upcoming birthdays, anniversaries, or other events in my calendar or contact information?

If I search Hollywood.com for movie listings at the nearest movie theatre, why not automatically add the theatre to my address book, complete with directions, or schedule a movie on my calendar? Why not enable me, at my own direction, to send this information to my buddy list as an invitation to join me to catch a flick?

As the image resolution produced by camera phones hits five mega pixels, why not enable me to transmit my images for reprint at the local photo store?

These sorts of capabilities add value to advertising that's specific to the device you're using.

In the United States, the Hear Music Coffeehouse in Santa Monica is a first-of-its-kind record store that combines a Starbucks coffee house with a music listening bar. Customers can sip their double half-caff soy latte and consult one of seventy Hewlett-Packard tablet PCs to peruse up to 20,000 songs, complete with artist interviews, reviews, and more. They can then build their own music compilation, and have it burned onto a CD while they wait.

While today the devices are tethered to the back-end system, and the experience is controlled through store-owned devices, "it's really not a very big leap to imagine that people will come into Starbucks with their Wi-Fi–enabled devices, and start downloading songs, playlists, video clips, or whatever," says Gene Becker, program director for the Mobile and Media Systems Lab at Hewlett-Packard, which provides the gear for the store. "By 2010, when we're all carrying around multi-terabytes of storage in our pocket, and as bandwidths improve in terms of technology standards and speed, that sort of thing will be common place. The possibilities are endless."

#9: THINK YOUNG—TO A POINT

There is little doubt that consumers younger than twenty-five years old are the first ones adopting wireless as much more than just a way to place phone calls.

According to a study from the Pew Internet & American Life Project, the prototypical mobile Internet user belongs to a demographic group it calls "the young tech elite." Making up 6 percent of the U.S. population, the average member of this group is twenty-two years old, and is among the most likely to be engaged in the more interactive aspects of the Internet, such as downloading music and creating online content. To this group, "the cell phone is more important than the wireline phone, and e-mail is as important as telephonic communications,"[27] says the report. What's more, 22 percent of those 18- to 27-year-olds have used laptops with wireless connections at least once in a given month, compared to 17 percent of those ages 40 to 58.[28]

"Young people are communicating digitally and wirelessly across the spectrum," says Tim Rosta, vice president of trade marketing for Viacom's MTV unit. Indeed, MTV has responded to the burgeoning wireless revolution by launching its own mobile portal—called *MTV—where fans send text messages, play games, hear music clips, and download ringtones based on shows ranging from *The Newlyweds* to *Real World*. "We've got to be where our customers are—and increasingly, they're mobile."[29]

But this group may have competition coming up the ranks. According to research firm Telephia, two-thirds of mobile teens use, and nearly all express interest in using, data services such as SMS.[30] And while 12 percent of U.S. mobile users have taken a photo with a camera phone, nearly 30 percent of eighteen- to twenty-five-year-olds have done so.[31]

"It's not even a Generation Y thing—it's more the generation after them," says Wes Bray, chief operating officer of mobile marketing firm Hip Cricket. "For these kids under 12 today, who have grown up with the small screens of Game Boys, this may be the first device they own to surf the Web, and it's going to be a source of entertainment, education, and knowledge management as well as communication. It's already being described as 'interactive cable TV for the Millennial Generation.'"

Indeed, a study from the U.K.–based research firm Teleconomy reports that 10- to 14-year-olds, which it calls "m-agers," are so emotionally attached to their wireless devices, they say they can't live without them.[32]

"There is a whole revolution that's been going on now for the last couple of years in the way young people communicate with one another," says Ralph Simon, chairman of the industry trade association Mobile Entertainment Forum. "Companies like McDonald's and Coca-Cola are looking at this because they realize that this is really part of the lingua franca of modern lifestyles."

Not everyone agrees that mobile is strictly the purview of the young, however. Enpocket's Jonathan Linner, for instance, points to the success of an SMS promotion his firm launched to boost viewership of TV movies on Lifetime TV in the United States.

"We targeted those two groups considered least likely to respond to SMS—women and the over 50s," he says. As it turned out, 30 percent of those who received the messages tuned into Lifetime because of the campaign. "It turned out to be one of the most successful campaigns we've ever run."

In fact, Enpocket's own research shows that mobile phone usage overall peaks in the thirty-five to forty-nine age group, where 69 percent own cell phones.[33] What's more, the usage patterns in some wireless data applications are similar across age groups. Eighteen- and thirty-four-year-olds exhibit little difference in behavior when it comes to activities like downloading ringtones.[34]

"Forty-year-olds may not use text messaging as much, but they do use it," says Linner, adding that campaigns for boomer-skewing Volvo have performed well, too. "The campaigns we do tend to be more youth-oriented, but it's not because of the medium. It's because of advertisers' perception of the medium haven't yet caught up with reality."

#10: THERE'S NO TIME LIKE NOW

Will wireless make or break your marketing plans? Of course not. Will it give you a competitive advantage as a particularly powerful and uniquely personal touch point within your integrated marketing efforts? Absolutely. Like the early days of the wireline Internet, the marketers who master it first will be better positioned as more consumers venture into the mobile medium.

"The marketers who fail to keep up with wireless will fall behind rapidly," says Tchong. "The [wireline] Internet has already shown that there's interest in developing—and embracing—'cool wired brands,' and I think we're going to see that develop even more rapidly when everybody's cell phone is Web-enabled."

Still, Tchong and others caution, anytime you have a new medium, the most important thing is to set realistic goals. The fact is, most mobile marketing today reaches very small niche audiences. There's a novelty factor to wireless advertising that isn't going to last forever. And nobody really knows where the technology—and consumer appetites—will take us next.

"The truth is, we're really just in the experimentation phase of wireless advertising," says Forrester analyst Jim Nail. "No one really knows how it's going to play out in terms of what business models will work, and which ones will even be effective."

In fact, Nail warns companies to go slow.

"I don't think advertising agencies and most advertisers have really fully exploited [wireline] Internet advertising, e-mail marketing, and search marketing," he says. "For the next couple of years, they'd be much better off putting money into really learning how to use *that* medium effectively, rather than going off chasing the next new thing."

Excellent point. But others contend that this kind of thinking may be a luxury for many brands whose very existence depends on fostering an aura of hipness. "We're pitching mobile marketing in virtually every conversation we have with clients," says Carat Interactive's Peters. "I guarantee you, many of the hottest consumer brands are eyeing this space closely, and actively experimenting with it, to understand when it will be the right time to really blow this thing out—not only to drive up sales, but to position themselves as cutting-edge brands."

"It all depends on your industry and who your customers are," explains Ogilvy's Ricketts. "In some cases, failing to keep up with the mobile revolution may mean very little. In others, it may mean risking total and absolute irrelevancy."

Christopher Locke:
"Cluetrain Manifesto" for the Mobile Age

Not everyone believes mass-market advertising translates to the wireless world. Just ask renegade marketing strategist and dyspeptic malcontent Christopher Locke, coauthor of *The Cluetrain Manifesto: The End of Business as Usual*, and author of *Gonzo Marketing, Winning Through Worst Practices*.

The problem, says Locke, is that in an increasingly interconnected world of the wireline—and now, wireless—Internet, new communities of consumers are growing immune to corporate pitches and officially sanctioned marketing-speak, much less mainstream news and media.

As a result, "the artist formally known as advertising must do a 180," contends Locke. The goal is market advocacy—tapping into, listening to, and even forming alliances with emerging online and wireless markets, and transforming advertising from clever ways of saying, "I want your money" to "We share your interests."

From *The Cluetrain Manifesto, The End of Business As Usual*, by Christopher Locke, Rick Levine, Doc Searls, and David Weinberger. Courtesy of Perseus Books.

RICK MATHIESON: What do *Gonzo Marketing* and *Cluetrain Manifesto* mean in a mobile age where the Internet travels with us?

CHRISTOPHER LOCKE: The big shift here is away from one-way communications from large organizations—whether they were media organizations or big companies or the government, telling people, "This is the way it is." We've moved from broadcast to point-to-point, peer-to-peer, group-to-group, where it isn't just a question about beaming out advertising. It's people who can go where they want, buy what is attractive to them.

You had a little of this with the remote control and TV, which bothered the hell out of broadcasters at first—"What if they switch away from the ads?" Well, this is orders of magnitude beyond that.

Now, people are talking to each other about your statements, creating online networks about any particular topic they're passionate about, and saying, "Yeah, well, we don't buy it," or, "We have a different view," which you never had before the Internet.

The fact that people can communicate with each other, that they can deconstruct and analyze and comment on the official channels of communication, is shifting power away from companies and the media, and more to masses that are self-selecting into micromarkets.

Look at blogging. With the wireless Internet, you're starting to see a lot more real-time commentary and analysis that's flying by so fast that if you're outside of it, and you're just reading the newspaper, you're just getting the news, while another couple of million people have already compared it to ninety-six other events and cross-indexed them, whether it's the Middle East or whatever these folks are interested in.

RM: How does this shift hamper or help the objectives of marketers?

CL: Marketers are largely wedded to ideas that are intrinsic to the broadcast paradigm. They've never known anything else. From the perspective of gathering an audience in broadcast, you want the biggest possible audience. You want the highest Nielsen ratings. And from the perspective of advertisers, you want the real easy jingle. You want the vanilla message that can be delivered many, many, many times, and goes into your limbic system, so you go out like an android and buy Downey Fabric Softener.

Marketers have made the mistake of thinking the Internet is like TV, when there are fundamental differences of interconnection and intercommentary and conversation. This is a technology that enables person-to-person and many-to-many conversations, and those conversations really define and characterize the medium in a way that just doesn't bear a lot of resemblance to broadcast or television at all.

Marketers—television is what they knew, so they employed the same sort of techniques, the same sort of shotgun, get the message out there, get the key points, get them to click the animated banner with the monkey who's running back and forth, or whatever.

In the first blush, some of the techniques had a certain appeal because they were novelties. But the novelty wore off after the third time you'd clicked the monkey, and it was like, "Oh, I get it. This is just the same old crap," even with all this "permission marketing" stuff.

RM: In fact, you contend that online audiences are self-segmenting into micromarkets, where, as a marketer, you can't really approach them on your own agenda anymore. You have to talk to them about theirs.

CL: Yes. Used to be, to start a television station, or a radio station, you had to sign up these big sponsors with high-ticket items—car dealers, car companies, and so on. It worked in that medium. Here, the market is fragmented.

But what's happened is that the big companies just repeat the same stuff online as they do everywhere else. You have NBC, ABC, CBS, all hawking the same homogenized crap. But that's the beauty of the Internet. It's just not one place, it's scattered all over. And audiences dig around and turn each other on to places that they like: "Well, have you heard what this guy is saying, or that woman is blogging," and so on.

The community that you volitionally participate in is always more true than a segment a marketer places you in. And that's the power of these micromarkets. They're not demographic abstractions. They're actual communities of discourse. Communities that are really talking to each other, and are not based just on interest, but passionate interest in how to make clothes for your kid, or how to powerboat, or snowboard, or write Java code, or thousands and millions of other obsessions.

If you approach those kinds of communities saying, "Hey, buy our new tires for your SUV." It's like, "Huh? Where the f— k did you come from?" It's like a guy walking into a party where people are in little groups around the room, talking about stuff that they're interested in, and here comes the used car salesman who wants to tell you, "Hey, I'm with Joe's Pontiac, and boy, we've got some great specials this week." How long would that guy last at a party? They would throw him out the damn door.

RM: So what's the alternative? How can companies effectively communicate with, and capitalize on, these 'networks' or micromarkets?

CL: Start by looking inside your own company at interests that your employees have—at passions. Not about your product. Not about the nine-to-five work. But what are your people really interested in? What do they care about? What do they do with their spare time?

Find those interests, because they are intellectual capital

that has been left lying in the dirt, unrecognized. It's what they want to get the next paycheck for, so that they can go buy the motorboat, or the snowboard, or the trip to Vail to go skiing. Find those interests among your people. Figure out which ones would map into your market in general.

Then, go out on the Web and find similar passions and interests represented by Web sites that are doing a good job, that have a demonstrable ability to be engaging—funny, well-written, graphically adept—and form relationships with those sites. Give them money. Give them technical resources.

It's almost like third-world development, where you grow them and ink legal relationships with these Web sites, so that you can intersect the people inside your company with that outside network, so when people hook up together, they're not talking to shills from Ford or Motorola or whoever. They're talking to people that are talking the same language about stuff they're interested in, and by the way, they're also meeting actual real people in those companies that they begin to have a feel for.

At some point, people say, "Hey, I need help with this or that," and a conversation starts that can end in a big sale. Along the way, you'll probably earn the kind of brand equity you've always wanted, in a way you never expected.

There are people who are highly, highly motivated and enthusiastic about certain aspects of the world, and there are usually products or services relating to those people in some way or another. Take fly-fishing. Advertising fly-fishing stuff on television probably doesn't make a lot of sense. But online, a company can sponsor or underwrite a fly-fishing contest, seminars, or an excursion, or tips on the best fishing spots this week. That can be very powerful.

But trying to get a bunch of sites to adhere to your notion of what you want the customer to hear is trying to drive the square peg into the round hole with a bigger hammer. And if we're not careful, that's what will happen here. It used to be that really intelligent people saw what was going on and were attracted to the Internet because it was different. Now, you turn it on and it's not different at all. It's like turning on the television. Yeah, I can get my flight information faster, and I can get my news without having to get those wet newspapers off the front porch. But the really radical stuff that's possible in this medium is in danger of falling by the wayside.

It's so much more powerful to go to these sites that are out there, give them some money to help them make their trip. And in each case, the money is a tiny fraction of what it would cost to do traditional advertising. It's about going out there to build goodwill, to build relationships, to build, ultimately, not just a place to advertise, but a place to participate in those communities, and bring new ideas into your company—real intellectual capital—and to get people really understanding what the company is doing, rather than just saying, "Buy my product."

RM: How will the mobile Internet give this trend pervasiveness?

CL: As the connection gets more ubiquitous, as you're freed from the desktop, as you have the ability to be more constantly connected, you can tap into your network anytime.

It's getting easier to go to your blogger, and say, "Hey, I'm at the corner of Walk and Don't Walk in New York City, and I'm looking for a good Chinese restaurant." It's fast enough that six people could come back and say, "Oh, you've got to go to Hop Sing's."

That's getting closer to real time, and guess what? It's more fun. Because somebody else that you trust can say, "Oh, you know, Charlie's telling you to go to Hop Sing's, but actually, that sucks. What you really want to do is walk three more blocks and take a left, and go to this other place that nobody knows about, but it's fantastic."

It's like an instant, always-on community giving you information that you trust because you've trusted them in other areas.

RM: A reputation system built on some kind of 21st-century version of the Old Boys' Club?

CL: Yes, that's a good analogy. Or The Alumni Association. You go to a new city, and you say, "Charles, where do you think we can get a good cigar?" You're going to trust Charles because he's from your class. You've got more tie-in to him than if he's some guy wearing a bow tie talking at you too loud.

RM: Hmmm . . . sounds great, but it's so grassroots. Is going Gonzo really a viable marketing strategy?

CL: No company in its right mind is going to shift its entire media budget to Gonzo Marketing.

But a lot of companies are spending a lot of money on corporate Web sites and not really getting much out of it. They can't take these sites down. It would be like being delisted on the stock market. It would be very bad, so they are hostage to paying lots of money to keep these sites up. They're not meeting their ROI expectations at all, and so what are they going to do?

I think a lot of these companies are scanning the horizon for alternatives. Gonzo Marketing is a really scary alternative. I think the classic company that is more desperate and has smarter folks is going to pick a few test steps to check this out, and I think they're going to do it very quietly.

This is not something you can do by formula, by algorithm. You're really going to have work by trial and error. On the other hand, I think Gonzo Marketing is only alternative because the dynamics that are embedded inherently in the medium are absolutely nonnegotiable.

Unfortunately, many companies are out there trying to

shove their view on these communities, and I'm disappointed in what I've seen in terms of what could have been done, and what has been done. If we're not careful, it will be more like Disney World than it is like the United Nations. I don't know which one is more of a joke.

TRAIN OF THOUGHT

The Cluetrain Manifesto burst onto the scene as ninety-five theses on the Web, and became a bestselling book that challenged corporate assumptions about business in the digital world. As that world goes wireless, a little *Cluetrain*, revisited:

▶ Markets are conversations.

▶ Markets consist of human beings, not demographic sectors.

▶ Conversations among human beings *sound* human. They are conducted in a human voice.

▶ The Internet is enabling conversations among human beings that were simply not possible in the era of mass media.

▶ As a result, markets are getting smarter, more informed, more organized. Participation in a networked market changes people fundamentally.

▶ People in networked markets have figured out that they get far better information and support from one another than from vendors.

▶ There are no secrets. The networked market knows more than companies do about their own products. And whether the news is good or bad, they tell everyone.

▶ Corporations do not speak in the same voice as these new networked conversations. To their intended online audiences, companies sound hollow, flat, literally inhuman.

▶ In just a few more years, the current homogenized "voice" of business—the sound of mission statements and brochures—will seem as contrived and artificial as the language of the 18th-century French court.

▶ Companies that assume online markets are the same markets that used to watch their ads on television are kidding themselves.

▶ Companies can now communicate with their markets directly. If they blow it, it could be their last chance.

▶ Companies need to realize their markets are often laughing. At them.

CHAPTER THREE

Dialing for Dollars

M-Commerce Puts Sales in Motion

What would Norma Desmond make of the mobile revolution?

In the Hollywood classic *Sunset Boulevard*, when the silent-film star is told she "used to be big," she famously retorts: "I am big. It's the pictures that got small."

These days, they're getting even smaller.

In their continuing efforts to reach increasingly elusive young audiences, Hollywood studios and entertainment companies are rapidly launching new mobile initiatives aimed at bringing their battle for eyeballs to the postage-sized screens of mobile devices. We've already discussed how the entertainment industry has been especially adept at using the mobile medium to promote its music, movies, and television shows. Thing is, they're also making money—and lots of it—as consumers discover they can do a lot more than just talk with their cell phones.

"Hollywood's gone wireless," says Gary Stein, a senior analyst with Jupiter Research. "The entertainment industry is one of the few sectors that's really seeing some success with some of the best uses of wireless."[1]

HOLLYWOOD @ HAND

Inspired by the blockbuster performance of the ongoing mobile promotion for *American Idol*, the race to leverage pop culture icons into the mobile medium spans the entire entertainment industry, from movie and television studios to major record labels and game producers.

Indeed, from *The Fantastic Four* to *Star Wars: Episode III* to *Kong*, every major movie campaign these days seems to have some kind of "m-commerce" tie-in—selling Ben Grim screen graphics, Jedi ringtones, Kong screen savers, and more.

Television networks are doing the same: Comedy Central has rolled out a host of offerings for wireless subscribers, including games, SMS jokes, news alerts, and voice greetings featuring characters from its popular shows *Crank Yankers, South Park,* and *Drawn Together*.

Food Network delivers bite-sized recipes over mobile phones to harried chefs, shoppers, and weekend meal planners. Subscribers get high-quality recipes from some of the television network's most celebrated foodies, from Emeril to the Iron Chef, as well as how-to tips and techniques for planning, preparing, and serving up taste-tempting meals.

And Fox Sports delivers "enhanced television" services during select National Football League broadcasts that allow fans to participate in live polls and trivia. On-air questions and polls are posted live via television, along with a SMS short code to respond. Poll results are tabulated in real-time, with results broadcast on-air. And participants are often offered games and graphics tied to the event for a fee. ABC-TV has done the same for NCAA college football. And Major League Baseball is staking out its own wireless front. In addition to sports scores, audio feeds, and $2.49 logos, MLB.com is also exploring the ability to sell direct video feeds to cell phone users for $7.99 per month. See Figure 3-1.

This premium content can be unique to the medium—content and services like Vindigo, Click2Music, and Buzztime Trivia, for instance. But today, the most popular offerings stem from existing

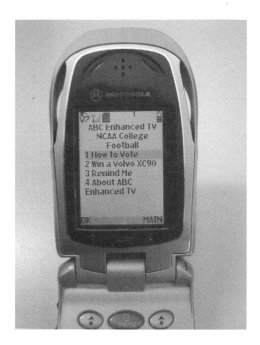

Figure 3-1. Services like ABC's Enhanced TV offers live voting via SMS/text messaging–enabled cell phones as a way to reach a new generation of young, tech-savvy viewers, who expect to interact with the shows they love. Photo: Proteus.

entertainment properties—from Nickelodeon to Marvel Comics to *Bloomberg News* to *Cosmo Girl Mobile* to Fox Sports and more.

"I think it has to do with a preexisting brand affinity," says Brian Levin, president of Mobliss, the mobile solutions provider behind *Idol*, as well as wireless promotions and games for such properties as *Family Feud*.[2]

Either way, the attraction is undeniable: At $1 to $3 a pop for some digital games, songs, trinkets, and even some SMS interactions—and $1 to $10 for monthly subscriptions to these and other forms of premium content—these m-commerce curios are raking in over $3 billion a year.

"By 2008, we're probably talking between $5 billion to $10 billion spent on premium content," says Adam Zawel, a Yankee Group analyst who tracks mobile entertainment.

With that in mind, the entertainment industry is already pumping $50 million into programs focused on m-commerce—a figure that will top $130 million in 2007, says Zawel. That's 5 to 10 percent of the total amount that studio marketers will earmark for all interactive projects combined, including the wireline Internet.[3]

There's a good reason for entertainment's robust interest in wireless. Most movies, TV shows, and popular music are aimed at the same pool populated by the most lucrative wireless subscribers: 12- to 24-four-year-old hipsters texting their way through adolescence, and star-struck grownups with nothing left to rebel against but their waistlines and a full head of hair.

Carriers are cashing into the trend, too. As the primary gatekeeper to mobile subscribers, carriers get a slice of the revenue each time a teenager downloads a ringtone of Lil' Flip's "Sunshine," plays the *BotFighter* mobile game, or surfs a porn site.

Wireless carriers are even selling television itself. Sprint PCS has made a bet that a large number of its 5 million subscribers will want to catch their favorite shows on the tiny screen of their wireless handsets in those distressingly rare moments when there's not a 52-inch flat-panel television in sight. The Kansas City, Missouri–based cell phone carrier was the first mobile operator in the United States to offer live digital television via cell phones with a service called MobiTV, which streams sixteen cable television channels live to subscribers for $9.99 a month, in addition to regular cellular subscription fees.

That means consumers can flip on their cell phones and tune into a Chris Matthews scream fest on MSNBC, the raucous rumblings of *Dinosaur Planet* on Discovery, or even Paige Davis and the deleterious decorators of *Trading Spaces* on TLC.

Working with mobile content network 1KTV, the carrier has even launched the first original television show created specifically for delivery via wireless handsets. Based on an early Web-based serial, *The Spot* features the daily lives of five twenty-somethings living in a seven-bedroom beach house in Santa Monica, and is touted as the first drama series for wireless to use writers, actors, and videographers, just as a regular television show does.

Now, you might be thinking: Who wants to watch television on a 1.5- by 2-inch screen? After all, if "mobile television" has an antecedent, isn't it the ill-fated Sony Watchman—that overhyped contraption from the 1980s that eventually went the way of mullets, leg warmers, and Members Only jackets?

Think again. While Sprint is mum on specifics, Paul Scanlon, vice president of Idetec, the solutions company behind two of

Sprint PCS's most popular television services, says subscriptions have sold faster than you can say "must-see TV."[4] It's so popular, Cingular Wireless has picked up the service, too.

Indeed, the idea is catching on. For about $15 per month, Verizon's V Cast service delivers an original, mobile phone-only spin-off of 20th Century Fox's TV hit *24,* called *24: Conspiracy.* Launched in early 2005, the V Cast service also offers one-minute "mobisodes" based on Paris Hilton's *The Simple Life: Interns,* as well as two new original mobile series, the salacious soap *The Sunset Hotel,* and an "unscripted drama" called *Love and Hate.*

"The cell phone is increasingly becoming an entertainment device—maybe as rich as the proverbial third screen—television, PC, and mobile," says Larry Shapiro, vice president of business development and operations for The Walt Disney Internet Group. In Japan, for instance, Disney has over 4 million subscribers who spend around $3 U.S. per month for premium content from Disney Mobile, which includes packages of ringtones, wallpaper, games, and other content based on properties from *The Little Mermaid* to *The Incredibles*—as well as mobile news feeds for ESPN and ABC News and the first 3D game for mobile phones, *Tron 2.0: Light Cycles.* Its mobile offerings are beginning to find an audience in the United States, too. Disney won't reveal numbers, but prospects are so good, that by the end of the decade, Shapiro says, the Mouse House could potentially start selling cell phones and mobile service under its own brand name, competing against the likes of Sprint, T-Mobile, Cingular, and others.

Yet while digital content may be getting all the attention today, another form of wireless transaction could have a more profound impact in coming years.

E-COMMERCE, UNLEASHED

M-Commerce is, quite simply, commerce conducted using a mobile handset. It is the mobile equivalent of e-commerce. That can mean the ability to download the kind of premium content described above, with charges added to your cell phone bill. Or it can mean a kind of "m-wallet," where you can purchase goods in the physical world and have it charged to a prepaid account, a credit card, or as a debit on your phone bill.

As we mentioned, in many parts of Asia, and a few places in Europe, this means the ability to point your phone at a vending machine, for example, to pay for snacks.

In Japan, "smart card" technology embedded in many new cell phones is designed to store money or credit card information. Consumers can make purchases at participating retailers, and can check their balances by logging onto the Internet using their phones or a wireline Web connection. Some models even include a remote-control locking system for disabling the phone if it is stolen or lost.[5]

In Europe, T-Mobile and solutions provider Encorus have developed a mobile wallet for purchases made with merchants who partner with the carrier, with charges billed to a credit card. And IBM, Visa, and Upaid have launched a system that uses SMS messages to authorize the transfer of funds. Meanwhile, a consortium of carriers, including Orange, T-Mobile, Vodaphone, and others have created a cross-carrier service called Simpay that enables mobile consumers to place purchases using their phones. Though the system was initially created for purchases of digital content, it is actively expanding to real-world stores.

M-Commerce as a concept has also produced variants that include "l-commerce"—for location-based commerce (think the Latte Scenario) and "v-commerce," for voice-enabled automated commerce (the equivalent of a dialing a call center to make a purchase).

Worldwide, m-commerce accounts for less than 2 percent of all online sales, which, in turn, accounts for about 1 percent of all retail sales.[6] While many parts of Asia and Europe are nuts for this stuff, m-commerce as a concept has laid fallow in the United States, with issues swirling around the interoperability of devices and networks, a lack of participating retailers, and general consumer distrust of wireless communications as a transaction medium. According to one study conducted by the Boston Consulting Group, for instance, 74 percent of Americans expressed concerns about sending credit card information over mobile networks, though the use of "micropayments" (those charges made to your cell phone bill) appears to be taking off in Europe and Japan.[7] British research firm Juniper estimates that the average Western European will make approximately twenty-eight such transactions per year by 2009.[8]

These and other business models are beginning to gain traction for a growing number of U.S. consumers looking for a whole new level of speed and convenience.

NO WIRES, NO WAITING

Call it the mobile Web's killer appetite. Customers at dozens of Washington, D.C.–area fast food restaurants can order food, beverages, and more through their cell phones. As simple as entering an SMS short code, fast food devotees can order their favorite meals as they drive through town and have it waiting, piping hot, at a special wait-free, cash-free pickup area—faster than you can say "Smokehouse Bacon Cheddar Burger, Large Garlic Fries, and a Super-Size Diet Coke."

The service, called WaitLess.com, represents a new generation of mobile services that has fast food junkies—and their favorite restaurants—salivating.

"You don't even need a parking spot," says Harri Ihanainen, CEO of ZonePay, Inc., the company behind the service. "You're in and out of the restaurant in half a minute."

Launched in 2002, WaitLess has signed up over eighty restaurants for the service, and hopes to expand to fifty cities by 2007. Fifteen Subway franchises and four Baja Fresh stores are among the firm's clientele.

Fuddruckers is testing the concept in seven locations. If it takes off, the popular custom burger chain could roll out the service to all of its 203 corporate and franchise-owned locations nationwide. At stake: continued success in a $115 billion fast food industry,[9] which sees $12 billion in annual sales from telephone orders alone.[10]

In fact, the entire industry is wondering: Will consumers eat up the ability to order food on the wireless Web? After all, why not just call in the order?

Well, forget speed dial, botched orders, and interminable holds: WaitLess's interface cuts ordering time down from minutes to mere moments. And a line-free experience can make a big difference in the hypercompetitive world of fast food.

"These restaurants get a lunch crowd, and every day, they get people who show up at their door and say, 'Forget it: I'm not going to wait twenty minutes to get my Subway sandwich,'" says Ihanainen.

Users sign up at the WaitLess.com Web site and fill out credit card information or select a prepaid option. They then enter as many individual meal profiles as they want—such as a favorite lunch order for the whole office, dinner for the kids at home, or treating the softball team after a game.

Once profiles are completed, users can place orders from the Web site, or from their cell phones, with just a few clicks—often within ten seconds or less. The company is even working on a solution that would enable customers to send preset SMS codes, so cell phone ordering takes less than three seconds. Today, most users access the service through a wireline Web site; about 15 percent of customers use the cell phone option. "It's growing all the time," says Ihanainen.

PIN codes protect consumers from the possibility of someone stealing their phones and placing orders. And WaitLess represents a minimal investment for restaurants. Systems—which include software for integrating with the restaurant's existing POS solutions—can be set up for about $1,000, though participating locations have to commit to express checkout for users. Beyond setup costs, Wait-Less collects a small portion of the revenues from each order.

Here's where things get interesting: The data collected by the system also offers powerful profiling opportunities. For instance, when a regular once-a-week customer drops off for, say, three weeks, a special offer—half-off their next order, perhaps—can be sent to him via e-mail or SMS.

Finally, "restaurants know who their customers are—real CRM

information," says Ihanainen. "They know where they're coming from, and they can act on that information."

Still, early tests of such a concept for Domino's Pizza were considered by many to be a spectacular flop. "For a consumer to be able to tap directly into the POS system and order without having to speak to an agent cuts significant cost from the restaurant," says Craig Shapiro, director of wireless services for mobile solutions firm Proteus, which was involved in a number of tests with Domino's. "But what we found is that consumers really would prefer to just dial the phone number."

"Our research showed that there isn't a high awareness for mobile commerce," says Mathew Piette, a spokesperson for Motorola, a technology provider for one of the tests, called PizzaCast.[11] "People don't yet understand the value proposition—that they can buy stuff via the mobile Web."

Even when they gravitated to such services, people didn't like having to set up a different account for each individual restaurant.

"As a consumer, I'm not going to sign up for a separate account with Subway, a separate account with Baja Fresh, a separate account with Fuddruckers," says Ihanainen.

And he's right, of course. No one would.

By contrast, WaitLess is an independent service that enables instant ordering from a host of restaurants; you set up an account once, and can order from any of your favorite eateries.

In fact, it is in many ways an excellent example of what 1:1 marketing guru Don Peppers calls a "Data Aggregation Agent"—a concept whereby a trusted third party handles transactions on behalf of a consumer, independent of any store or restaurant, without revealing personal credit or banking information. With WaitLess, the transaction is blind to the restaurant; credit card numbers and personal information never reach them, and any special offers the restaurant wants to promote are coordinated through WaitLess.

"We're like eBay, building a community of users that don't want to send their credit card information," says Ihanainen, referring to eBay's ability to let buyers and sellers conduct transactions via PayPal. Ihanainen adds that the company hopes to branch out to other service categories as well, including video rentals, taxi service, and dry cleaning.

In short: While the most effective models for m-commerce have to be perfected, this is a glimpse of things to come.

THE PERFECT STORM

The North Carolina Hurricanes hockey team has long enjoyed a great deal of success with m-commerce, enabling fans to purchase tickets through Web-enabled cell phones and PDAs via the team's wireless Web site, Canes1.com.

The team was an early pioneer in U.S.–based wireless marketing, having launched the National Hockey League's first wireless ad campaign and reportedly generating a 15 percent response rate on around 10,000 impressions—ads delivered to individual wireless users—at around $40 to $80 per thousand ad impressions. Around 8 percent of respondents ended up buying tickets, saving $5 on admission as part of the promotion.

The ads enticed users to initiate a "call-through," the wireless equivalent of a "click through." Once initiated, the call-throughs connected users to the team's ticket office, where they were able to buy tickets.

"It's not enough to wait for someone to sit in front of their TV or turn on their computer anymore," says Howard Sadel, the team's director of new media and graphic communications. "You need to reach them on the road, in the airport, and on the go."

The test campaign went well, and Sadel says the team will do more in the future. But just the same, Sadel has found a more immediate—and more lucrative—way to capitalize on m-commerce.

Working with Sun Microsystems and other partners, the team revamped Canes1.com to enable fans to participate in interactive trivia during live hockey games. They can vote for MVPs, play fantasy hockey games, have food delivered to their seats, augment their viewing experience with real-time scores, stats, and game information, and bid in auctions for memorabilia. They can also still check out news and purchase tickets, anywhere, anytime. But the most compelling venue for this experience is in-stadium, during a game, where promotions and interactivity with fans take center stage—complete with Jumbotron voting, videogame scores, and auction promotions—making this an early form of "l-commerce," or commerce based on location.

About 10,000 to 12,000 fans participate in these wireless activities every season. That's a small fraction of the 1.2 to 1.8 million fans who take part via the team's wireline Internet site. But the number is growing.

And while the team and league have been buffeted by a bitter labor dispute that resulted in the cancellation of the 2005 hockey season, wireless promises to help wow fans in seasons to come.

"Wireless just makes sense because of how the fan experience can be enhanced," says Sadel. "From being able to sit in your seat and order food, to playing the games, to buying tickets, to outbound promotions and sports scores sent directly to fans wherever they are, it just has huge potential. At some point, it becomes more powerful than the Web site, no doubt."

Next up: Sadel hopes to blanket the surrounding neighborhood with WiMax to "narrowcast" premium Canes content—delivering digital content to specific recipients, in this case local sports bars, restaurants, and other retail partners—so he can further fuel fandemonium. By 2012, he says, we all may have a level of connectivity, "where my cell phone automatically interfaces with my car when I get in, and it'll deliver narrowcast audio, and sooner after that, video, directly to screens or speakers in my car. It's not that far off."

THAT'S THE TICKET

Moviefone, a service of America Online, will no doubt use these and other capabilities to get you out of the car and into a Cineplex. Moviefone's revamped mobile site, launched summer 2005, enables movie fans to check movie listings, read reviews, find the nearest theater, and preorder tickets.

"I think the real benefit for users is the ability not only to get theater information and show times, but also to convert that information, with a couple of clicks, into buying a ticket," says Lowell Winer, senior business development manager for America Online's entertainment properties. Like WaitLess.com, Moviefone enables users to set up an account by entering credit card information through a Web portal. When they go to buy a ticket from their cell phone, an encrypted authentication process matches the phone with the account to complete the transaction.

An earlier version of the service offered local movie listings, but lacked the m-commerce capabilities that would make it a true companion to Moviefone's telephone and Web-based services. Winer hopes that future phases of the service's evolution will include geo-location capabilities that offer directions to the theater relative to the location of the device, full video display of movie trailers, and even a community for fan-based movie commentary, and SMS–based alerts about coming attractions.

"As the mobile handset becomes more of a PC–[like] device, and there's browsing and an experience of multimedia content, this becomes a good exercise for us to learn about mobile data and learn about what consumers want," he says. "I would imagine this won't be the last asset [AOL] deploys on a handset."

According to Winer, wireless is a natural extension of Moviefone's other Web- and voice-based offerings.

"Some consumers just don't like have to deal with integrated voice response systems," he says, referring to the "for local listing, press three, to purchase tickets, press nine" element of the telephony experience. "It takes longer, and it can be a frustrating experience, especially when you're punching in your credit card number to buy a ticket, whereas with this, you're already authenticated, and it's just a much cleaner, simpler experience."

In fact, Moviefone has seen transactions via its Web site surpass its venerable voice service, increasing to 12 million unique monthly visitors, or roughly 60 percent of its user base. About 5 percent of all users go on to purchase advance tickets through one of the

Moviefone venues. Winer hopes wireless will increase that percentage, and help keep the service one step ahead of the competition, including Fandango, Hollywood.com, and others.

"Irrespective of competition, Moviefone is one of the top couple of [AOL] products that we're interested in launching into the mobile space, simply because it's a utility on the go," he says. "The competitive environment just makes it that much more interesting."

VOX HUMONGOUS

Winer's misgivings notwithstanding, Moviefone's original medium—automated voice telephony—is also experiencing an overhaul. While mostly unknown by name, "v-commerce," for "voice commerce," could easily be the most widely adopted form of mobile transaction in the United States. And it's about to get much, much better as marketers get set to roll out new speech-enabled services.

"The natural evolution of the Web is to include and encompass voice," says industry analyst Rob Enderle.

Today, AOL By Phone enables users to access e-mail to have messages read back to them. In the future, these mobile Web services will enable automobiles to tell you when you're running low on gas, and then direct you to the nearest service station. Or voice-based applications that translate conversations between two or more people speaking completely different languages.

In the 1990s, a series of desultory efforts to create compelling voice-based solutions resulted in often disappointing solutions with acronyms including VRU (voice response unit), IVR (the dreaded interactive voice recognition), and CTI (computer telephony interaction).

The problem with a lot of these systems is that you have to push buttons on the keypad and make your way through decision trees to get to the layer of information you want. Often, the process becomes very irritating, very fast.

Advanced speech-recognition solutions based on VoiceXML (XML stands for Extensible Markup Language, which enables different types of computers and systems to interoperate) and other standards allow those decision trees to be flattened so that you can state exactly what you want, and the system gets it to you fast. As an interface model, experts say, these solutions keep the user interested in the application—and it's already a hit with companies and consumers alike.

Moviefone competitor Fandango, for instance, uses solutions from Mountain View, California–based Tellme Networks, to enable callers to use their voice to order tickets, instead of pushing buttons. The system also uses the caller's area code and phone number to give directions to the nearest theater based on the caller's location.

Virgin Atlantic, meanwhile, offers a dedicated voice-based flight service that responds to customers' inquiries and enables passengers to rapidly obtain information about flight departure and arrival times. The service, used by half a million customers per year, allows Virgin Atlantic's call center agents to spend more time with customers that have more complex inquiries.

And in an effort to reduce staffing costs and do away with a cumbersome touch-tone phone system, UBS, one of the leading private banking services worldwide, used technologies from Nuance to create an automated system that could understand callers, regardless of accent, and deliver an excellent user experience in a personalized voice. The new system enables UBS's 4 million customers, anywhere, anytime, to check bank balances, make transactions, transfer funds, and find out the latest information on a selection of European and American equities, just by speaking naturally into their phone—cell phone or otherwise. The system even features custom, natural-voice personas, allowing the dialogue to have a conversational style.

"The idea is to design the interface so that the callers have a good experience and don't need to talk to a live agent," says Marcello Typrin, group product marketing manager for speech solution provider Nuance. "But in the event they do, then there's certainly a way for them to get there."

Nuance's automated personas come with complete back stories and accents that provide a personality to voice applications.

"It's great in terms of communicating a brand," says Typrin. "A human can now talk to a machine and have it feel a lot more like natural conversation."

The market for such solutions is expected to be huge. Companies that enable customers and employees to access automated v-commerce systems, instead of having to talk to a live operator, experience a 10 to 30 percent decrease in operational expenditures for support functions, according to Forrester Research.[12]

There's even evidence that consumers like the choice. Recent industry studies indicate that 50 percent of consumers approve of voice-based self-service as an alternative to live operators—as long as it's easy to access one, if needed.[13]

Meanwhile, new "multimodal" technologies may make v-commerce solutions even more powerful.

In the future, such solutions might enable computer servers to sense the type of device a person is using to reach a company's Web site or contact center—cell phone, PDA, or PC. The user would then use voice, stylus, or keypad, whichever is most convenient at the time.

Still, with roughly 40 percent of contact center calls now originating from cell phones, voice may not be a total replacement for a keyboard or stylus, but it's still the original—and ultimate—user interface.

"Speech is the most natural form of communication that there is, and everyone knows how to do it," says James Mastan, director of marketing for Microsoft's speech technology group. "By enabling computing devices to interact with a human through speech, you can have a much richer interaction with a computer. And customers will be more satisfied, because they can actually get things done that they couldn't get done before."

Of course, it may be a while before consumers gravitate toward using their phones to place transactions, voice, location, or otherwise. For the rest of this decade, experts say, the real money in m-commerce is expected to remain in digital content delivered directly to handsets. In fact, its two most popular forms—mobile music and games—are absolutely booming.

PUTTIN' ON THE HITS

It's nothing short of ironic. While the global music industry finds itself locked in a pitched battle against rampant Internet piracy, it's making a killing with sales of ringtones.

Long the prime symbol of cell phone personalization among Gen-Y hipsters, the ubiquitous, mono- and polyphonic sound bites long ago began replacing the standard ring of incoming calls with electronic imitations of the hit pop single du jour.

In the U.S. market, for instance, 15.7 percent of cell phone subscribers use ringtones, while 65 percent rate ringtone functionality as a primary driver for upgrading a handset, according to research firm Telephia.[14] Already, that translates to over $250 million in sales in the United States, and could easily translate into 54.3 million U.S. ringtone subscribers by 2007, up from 4.8 million in 2002, according to estimates from International Data Corporation.[15]

As it turns out, at up to $2.50 a download, ringtones for new hits from the likes of OutKast, Missy Elliot, and Ludacris represent incremental income even file swap-fearing music labels can't resist—accounting for somewhere between $2.3 billion[16] to $3.5 billion[17] in sales worldwide. That's roughly equivalent to 5 to 10 percent of the entire, $32.5 billion global music market.[18]

Continuing the irony, consumers who show reservations about downloading full music tracks at 99 cents per song at iTunes, or $14.95 a month for unlimited subscriptions at Napster To Go, seem to feel no compunction about downloading 15-second clips—often rendered with electronic beeps and blurbs—at two to four times the price.

To cash in on the trend, MTV and Warner Bros. have teamed up to sell new music and voice greeting ringtones from neo-grunge band Green Day and others. "We're in the culture with each and every one of our artists," Tom Whalley, the chairman of the Warner Bros. label, told the *New York Times*.[19] "The ringtone can help connect that fan to the artist if it's done with taste." For Green Day, that tasteful approach to marketing includes band members belching and cursing, as well as Mike Dirnt, the band's bassist, shouting, "It's your mother. I know. She's with me."

"You can see by the type of music genres, that the younger you go, the more interesting it is," says Jupiter analyst Avi Gardner. "While it's entirely possible that fifty-five-year-old white men are downloading hip-hop, whatever is popular tends to show up in ringtones."

Music marketers are making the most of it. Hip-hop star 50 Cent, a perennial top-seller among ringtone aficionados, has signed a deal making etailer Zingy.com the exclusive distributor of 50 Cent ringtones, voicemail greetings, and more.[20]

Sales of the thirty-second ringtone to 50 Cent's "In Da Club" eclipsed sales of the digital song, despite the fact that the clip contained no lyrics and was twice the 99-cent cost of buying the ditty via iTunes.[21]

"Ringtones are the new single," says industry expert Shawn Conahan, a former president of mobile content firm Moviso. "Given the state of the traditional business model for the record labels, this sort of new media model is starting to look very attractive."[22]

In fact, ringtones already outsell singles in Britain. And they're now charted, top-20 style, by *Music Week* in the UK, and by *Billboard* in the United States.[23] More amazing: These acoustic avatars of mass individualism are already taking a backseat to another aural phenomenon: the "ringback tone."

PERSONAL CALLS

As first reported by the *Wall Street Journal*, NMS Communications, a Framingham, Massachusetts–based wireless platform provider, and SK Telecom, a South Korean wireless carrier, first pioneered the new-fangled service feature. And it's quickly becoming a red-hot trend worldwide.

A ringtone, of course, broadcasts a ditty for all within earshot of a cell phone subscriber's incoming call. Ringbacks do the same thing for the subscriber's callers—replacing the traditional ringing sound a caller hears with a thirty-second music or voice clip.

"If you think about the psychology, you buy a ringtone for your phone so you can prove to people within fifteen feet of you when your phone rings that you're a cool person," says Brough Turner, senior vice president of network solutions for NMS. "If you buy a ringback tone, you're proving to the people who are calling you that you're cool."

Indeed, Turner says adoption of ringbacks could quickly surpass ringtones for one simple reason: technology.

That's because ringtones require users to download and store sound clips on advanced handsets that are compatible with a specific carrier's network equipment and protocols.

But NMS's platform, called HearSay, resides on the carrier's servers, and can deliver ringbacks to any phone used to call the subscriber.

"Even people with rotary dial-up phones could play ringbacks for their callers," says Turner.

Subscribers provision their own ringbacks via their handsets, or through a traditional Web site, where they can select from a catalog of songs, typically aggregated by separate content companies.

Users can even match each song to caller ID, choosing a specific clip for individual callers—say, 'Lil Romeo for the peeps and Matchbox 20 for parental types. When callers dial up a subscriber, the server simply matches up the title to the caller and delivers the clip.

What's more, the sound quality for ringbacks is comparable to that of a voice mail—a big advantage over the quaintly retro sound of ringtones.

In addition to Zingy, sites like yourmobile, ringtones.com, and numerous carrier sites offer ringtones and, increasingly, ringbacks, usually on a subscription basis for a certain number of songs, or as individual downloads. And new offerings called "Razzes," from San Francisco–based Phonebites, take it all a step further by enabling users to insert song clips and sound bites directly into phone conversations.

"Music is such a part of youth culture," says Yankee Group analyst Linda Barrabe. "This is a perfect fit for certain portions of the market who wouldn't mind paying $2 to $5 monthly for a certain number of music options."[24]

The next major trend: entire songs downloaded to your handset. In early 2005, Apple announced plans to offer its popular iTunes digital music service to consumers with Motorola cell phones.[25] And other new MP3/cell phone hybrids hit the market every day.

Solutions like NMS's HearSay may have a leg up, according to Turner. The same technology used to deliver ringbacks will soon be used to enable consumers to create audio albums that stream music—perhaps hundreds of songs—to mobile handsets. That could be a marked advantage over offerings that store songs on the device. The first proposed model for the Apple's cell phone–based service reportedly could store a dozen or so songs, though that will change as phones gain iPod-like storage capabilities.

However songs are delivered, the market is expected to be music to the industry's ears. According to a study by in-Stat/MDR, 11.4 percent of U.S. mobile subscribers are very or extremely interested in moving beyond basic ringtones to purchasing more full-featured music/audio services for delivery to their handsets—including news/talk content.[26]

Research firm Ovum, meanwhile, reports that by 2008 ringtones, ringback, and mobile song downloads could collectively top 28 percent of total music sales, including CDs and paid wireline downloads.[27]

Which means we haven't seen—or heard—the start of it.

GAMES PEOPLE PLAY

Call them pocket pastimes. Games to go. Or even fun on the run. By whatever name, a new breed of highly interactive wireless games is taking the industry by storm. And they could give Nintendo's Game Boy and Sony's Play Station Portable a run for their money.

"Entertainment is the ultimate killer app," says Scott Lahman, cofounder of Jamdat Mobile, which produces a host of games designed specifically for the mobile environment, including its popular *Jamdat Bowling*, as well as mobile extensions of brands like *Tony Hawk's Underground*, *Lord of the Rings: The Return of the King*, and *Jamdat NFL*. "Bad games don't drive usage. But a good game can get players hooked—and fast."[28]

Even console gaming giant Electronic Arts is getting in on the action. In mid-2005 the company leveraged many of its most venerable titles into the mobile medium—including *Tiger Woods PGA Tour*, *Madden Football*, and *Need for Speed*, among others. And it's easy to see why. According to research firm IDC, revenue for wireless gaming will grow from just under $160 million in 2003 to $1.7 billion by 2008.

Part of the boom is due to advances in mobile technology. When mobile games were first introduced, they mostly featured rudimentary graphics along the lines of *Pong* and *Asteroids*. With the advent of Java technology from Sun Microsystems, and BREW from Qualcomm, gaming experiences as rich as those on any console or portable game device became possible (not to mention profitable).

Mobile games, offered through cell phone carriers' main menus, enable players to go solo, or in some cases, challenge others in multiplayer tournaments.

"People want to play with other people," says Lahman. "They like to feel that they're outdoing another human."[29]

While hardcore console gamers spend hours getting to the next level of *Doom 3* or *Grand Theft Auto: Vice City*, most wireless games are played in mere minutes—while someone waits for a plane, or stands in a grocery store checkout line. But with so much wireless connectivity built right in, longer-form games are taking hold.

No wonder many portable gaming device manufacturers are adding new forms of wireless connectivity. The Nintendo DS, VIA Eve, and Sony PSP devices are outfitted with Wi-Fi connectivity to enable multiplayer gaming between devices, as well as with console.[30] One thing is certain: You can expect more forms of wireless connectivity by decade's end.

GET YOUR GAME ON

While ringtones and their ilk may prove most lucrative for movie, television, and recording studios, gaming is actually open to all marketers, not just those with games to sell.

Dubbed "branded entertainment," mobile games designed to feature specific products in starring roles can create immersive experiences for key demographic audiences. In *Jeep Off Road Jam*, for instance, players wiggle their Wrangler down trails and rough terrain. As they progress up levels, their Jeeps are upgraded to the Sport, Sahara, and, finally, the top-of-the-line Rubicon.

"Here's an opportunity where you can blend the brand into the entertainment experience, with rich graphics, color, and action," says Craig Holland, president and founder of mobile game maker Thumbworks, which was recently acquired by international mobile entertainment firm IN-FUSIO. It sure beats an SMS campaign."

Holland's company also produced *Suzuki Motocross Challenge*, which places players at the center of a championship motocross race featuring jumps, obstacles, and bonus points for aerial stunts.

"The bikes in the game are based on the real motorcycles, down to the color and the model numbers," says Holland. "Games are a really interesting alternative, because if you look at other types of media, advertising interrupts the entertainment experience—and when you're talking about a young male audience, guys are trying to get rid of that kind of stuff. [Branded games] make you part of that experience in a very powerful way."

Besides, there's money to be made—typically $3.99 to $5.99 per mobile game, says Holland.

Even when they're free, the ability to use mBranding can prove quite powerful. In PC-based gaming, more than 10 million people have downloaded *America's Army*, a first-person shooter game that the Army gives away as a rather desensitizing—and reportedly effective—recruitment tool. And the $40 *Full Spectrum Warrior* sets the action in Baghdad, where players take on Iraqi insurgents.[31]

A variant called "in-game branding" enables marketers of everything from movies to consumer-packaged goods to use gaming as a promotional tool. Imagine billboards and signage in popular games like *NBA Basketball One-on-One, Highway Racer, JAMDAT Racing,* or *Baseball Heroes of the MLBPAA,* where advertisers can hawk everything from soda pop to candy bars to music CDs to athletic shoes.

For DaimlerChrysler, in-game and branded game experiences have proven quite fruitful. Though the company doesn't break out numbers for results from mobile games, its overall "adver-game" initiative, which includes *Challenge* and the popular PC–based *Jeep 4x4: Trail of Life,* has resulted in hundreds of thousands of downloads. Approximately 40 percent of players report they're considering buying one of the company's vehicles.

"We're using electronic gaming to do what we've done with advertising throughout the ages—we're casting a net where the fish are schooling," says Joel Schlader, Chrysler Group's senior specialist for interactive marketing and gaming. "In some cases, gaming becomes a very good surrogate for a virtual test drive. One of the benefits of advertising through electronic gaming is that it's very interactive, and it's fun. You can arguably provide more realism with electronic games than you can with any other medium, other than being physically with the product. It's like a movie in that there is a story being told. But unlike a movie, the story has a different ending each time you play." See Figures 3-2 and 3-3.

Chrysler Group has also embedded advertising billboards in popular games like the *Tony Hawk Pro Skater* series of games. Indeed, the trend toward product placement is growing swiftly. In *Tom Clancy's Splinter Cell: Pandora Tomorrow,* success on one level of gameplay is contingent on the protagonist mastering a Sony Ericsson smart phone.[32] Spending on such in-game advertising has already reached $200 million a year worldwide, and could top $1 billion by 2008.[33]

Given the changing media consumption patterns of eighteen- to thirty-four-year-old men, in particular, this is no small matter. In

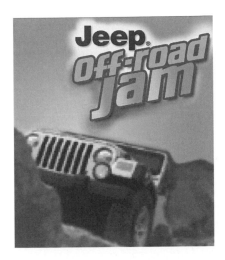

Figures 3-2 and 3-3. Games like Jeep Off Road Jam and Suzuki Motocross Challenge showcase the future of branded mobile entertainment. Photos: ThumbWorks.

the offline world, Nielsen Entertainment and game producer Activision have created a game-rating service similar to the venerable Nielsen TV service. Gamers who agree to participate use gear that tracks what games they're playing, what level they're on, and which in-game ads they're being exposed to, so advertisers can optimize their in-game ad space purchases at a level that's currently impossible with television.

Using new peer-to-peer solutions from New York–based Massive Inc., advertisers like Nike, DaimlerChrysler, and Intel even have the flexibility to serve up ads when players who are most likely to want their products are logged onto online games. "We can target specific demographics or even specific regions of the country," Richard Skeen, Massive's VP for advertising sales, told *Business 2.0.*[34]

That means if it's June, and you're at level three of *WWE Day of Reckoning*, you might see an ad for an upcoming summer blockbuster. If it's November, you might see an ad for holiday gift ideas. You may one day even be able to place a purchase.

And while the system currently only works with Massive's

wireline gaming network, similar functionality may one day come to wireless—and could even entail links to product information or even direct sales.

STAR ATTRACTIONS

That may be a while. Today, the content—music, games, graphics, and interactive communications—remains the major component of mBranding in general, and m-commerce in particular. And why not? Show business success has always been predicated on the pursuit of youth and the adoption of new technologies, from talkies to color movies to television to the Internet and beyond. It's no different in wireless.

"The entertainment industry is a very competitive business, and Hollywood has always been an early adopter of any new medium," says Jonathan Linner, CEO of Enpocket, which has produced mobile initiatives for several movies and TV shows.

"Hollywood is starting to pay attention to mobile because the results have been really incredible."

Or, as Norma Desmond might put it, m-commerce may finally be ready for its close-up.

Photo: Jeffrey Dodge Rogers

Gary Hamel:
Leading the (Wireless) Revolution

As chairman of international consulting firm Strategos, Gary Hamel is always in high demand.

His frequent speeches at marquee venues—including the World Economic Forum in Davos, the Fortune 500 CEO Roundtable, and Bill Gates's CEO Summit—make headlines worldwide. And his landmark books, including *Competing for the Future* and *Leading the Revolution* have hit over twenty best-seller lists. With *The Quest for Resilience: Building the Ultimate Competitive Advantage*, Hamel has cemented his reputation as the world's most sought-after business strategist.

It was Hamel, for instance, who helped counsel a 135-year-old Finnish rubber goods producer called Nokia as it altered course to become the world's number one manufacturer of mobile phones in less than a decade.

Over a twenty-year career, Hamel has helped management teams at some of the world's most prestigious companies create rule-breaking strategies that have generated billions of dollars in new wealth. His message to businesses on the cusp of the wireless age is as simple as it is powerful: Innovate—or else.

RICK MATHIESON: How will an always on, always available, wireless Internet—accessible from any device, anywhere—accelerate the pace of economic change? And what does it mean for companies and brands trying to keep up, or get ahead, in the emerging wireless age?

GARY HAMEL: You have to assess this trend along with a variety of technologies—broadband into the home, richer media, and others—that, together with wireless, will continue to be one of the primary forces accelerating change in our world.

Essentially, every industry on the planet is being reinvented from the customer backwards, and this involves something far more profound than simply being market-focused. It really means rethinking every aspect of the business through the lens of the customer's experience.

And you see places where this has begun to happen. A good example would be PayPal, which allows you, with enormous ease, to move money around the world. I think PayPal now has more registered users than any large bank has customers. You see it with technologies like personal video recorders that allow you to basically construct your own broadcast television network—and skip all of the advertising to boot.

Wireless technology is another powerful mechanism for reinventing the customer experience. It means, ultimately, that I will be able to watch television anywhere. As just one example, Samsung and others are working on integrating television reception into mobile phones. It also means that I would be able to transact business with any company—no matter where I am, day or night—irrespective of any land-line connection.

I do think, however, that there are a lot of people who expected that mobile phones would lead to a lot of location-specific services and location-specific advertising. I'm much more suspicious about this for the following reason.

I think that with an explosion of spam and pop-ups,

and all the other invasive means of inserting yourself into a customer's world, we are in the process of seeing a substantial backlash. And I believe that customers will, over the coming years, have more and more control over what messages they receive, and when and where they receive them, and it's going to be increasingly difficult for any company to take your attention hostage without you wanting that to happen.

Rather, businesses that are looking at wireless have to be asking not, "How do we use this to interrupt our customers?" Not, "How do we use it to capture their attention?" Instead, they should be asking, "How do we use it to directly address the frustrations and the concerns that get in the way of our customers having a completely fulfilling experience with our company?" I think if that's the motivation, then wireless will be a very powerful tool for changing when and where and how we buy.

RM: You assert that amid this technological revolution, companies that were built to last must now be rebuilt to change. How come?

GH: We've spent 100 years focusing on the problem of resource transformation. How do you transform input into output as efficiently as possible? But increasingly, there's an important additional challenge, which is a strategic transformation. And what we see when we look today at companies in the airline industry, the food industry, the software industry, the music industry, the pharmaceutical industry, we see many, many companies that are wrestling with a challenge of changing themselves and their business models in fairly deep and profound ways. Historically, such change only happens belatedly, in a crisis.

And these crises exert a very high cost in terms of employee morale, missed opportunities, shareholder wealth; and the challenge has to be that large organizations learn how to change themselves more frequently and more deeply with far less trauma.

In the Industrial Age, we assumed that a company and its business model were virtually synonymous. Xerox was a company that would sell and service copiers. Coca-Cola would be a company that would sell brown fizzy liquid, and so on. That kind of thinking can be toxic today.

Today, a company that cannot separate its sense of identity from any particular business model is not going to be able to outlive that business model. That's what you have seen in the last few years—literally hundreds of companies that didn't survive beyond their first strategy.

RM: What are the first steps a CEO and his team can take to start transforming a company, as you call it, into a "perpetual innovation machine" that can outlive its original business strategy?

GH: In many companies, there's a substantial rhetoric/reality gap around innovation. There's a lot of rhetoric at the top about how important innovation is. And this is understandable given the kind of debilitating effects of price-based hypercompetition. Everyone would like to believe there's some way out of that through innovation.

What we've learned is, A, you have to be capable of deconstructing your industry orthodoxies; you have to be able to challenge the beliefs that everybody else takes for granted. And B, you have to be very attuned to the new things that are changing our world, changes in demographics and circulation technology, and you particularly have to be looking for things that are changing that your competitors are not yet paying attention to. Not things that might change one day, but things that are already changing but have so far escaped unnoticed by your competitors, who may be looking elsewhere. Then, you have a chance to do something new to satisfy a need or a desire that your competitors have not yet even heard about.

[When Nokia was transforming itself into a cell phone manufacturer], for instance, all of its work was very much grounded in an understanding in the way the world was changing, and understanding the blind spots and orthodoxies of their competitors. Among all of those options and ideas, as we looked across them, there were some patterns that stood out very clearly.

One of those was there was an opportunity to make a phone that was much more fun, much more cool, much more easy to use than anything that had been done up until that time. You have to remember, the time we were doing this, the average Motorola phone was a fat black brick. And the idea of giving a phone a bigger user interface, of doing the phones in colors, putting in a menu-driven user interface—all of these things were relatively new ideas.

Another broad pattern that emerged was around making the phone something more than a voice device. They had this idea of using a phone as a terminal for making purchases, using it for text-based and multimedia-based purposes, perhaps using it one day for security. And that led to another whole vector of innovation, which they called "virtual presence." How do you think of the phone not simply as a communication device, but as a way that allows you to project your presence wherever you are, your presence as a business, reaching a consumer who wanted to make a purchase; your presence as a researcher, wanting to get some bit of information off the Web; whatever it might be.

So Nokia began looking at the mobile phone as "the remote control for life." And it was that set of insights that came to them at least four or five years before their competitors really began to understand the potential of the mobile phone to become a truly global consumer device.

Today, in every industry, businesses that are looking for direction on where to go next are discovering a world where consumers carrying around these wireless devices have new expectations of the way they will be served. And businesses are trying to figure out what that means to their industries.

The world of wireless may very well play a part in changing the kinds of products and services you offer, the way you interact with your customers—and when, where, and how you serve them—in ways that impact not just the brand experience, but your entire business model.

CHAPTER FOUR

A Moving Experience

The New World of Place-Based Marketing

Once again, the advertising world's most relevant work is being produced on Madison Avenue.

Or East 52nd Street. Or Riverside Drive, as the case may be.

Adapt Media of New York City is among the first companies to take advantage of new mobile solutions—including embedded GPS, ad server, wireless, and Web technologies—to enable a whole new form of advertising vehicle: mobile electronic billboards, mounted atop taxis, that display messages based on the cab's exact time and exact location.

"If Macy's wants to run a sale only during lunch time, they can announce it on every taxicab within a two-block radius between the hours of 11 A.M. and 1 P.M.," says Baruch Katz, the company's chief technology officer. "It's a whole new way to target a New York audience while they're on the move."

We've talked a lot about advertising and commerce via consumer handsets. But another, arguably more powerful form of mBranding is emerging in untethered, "place-based" marketing communications that capitalize on the power of wireless technology—most often without requiring consumer adoption of what we typically refer to as mobile devices.

"The service gives advertisers something they can't get anywhere else," says Katz. "We enable them, in real time, to modify their messages based on time and location."

Indeed, having expanded to over 500 cabs in just a few years of operation, Adapt's service—called ad|runner—has become a bona fide hit with New York's media elite.

The first advertiser to sign on was none other than ESPN, which uses the billboards to display real-time sports scores and to promote its flagship Sports Center TV program.

"It's hard enough to get people to notice your brand, much less think twice about it," says Justin Barocas of ad agency Anomaly, and former head of media planning for Wieden & Kennedy, ESPN's ad agency. "The taxi-tops are engaging and compel consumers to interact with ESPN's brand. They are a great example of 'participative media.'"

MTV has displayed its Music Video Award winners on taxis within moments of announcing them during its live, televised broadcasts.

And Time Warner Cable of New York and New Jersey used the taxi-tops to announce the availability of its RoadRunner high-speed Internet service and its DTV digital TV service on a street-by-street basis.

"The neat thing is, our cable or digital TV service may be available on one block or in one specific building, and we were able to target ads to people in those exact locations," says Harriet Novet, the company vice president of public affairs. "Being able to reach precise locations was a great way for us to break through the clutter that is walking across the street in New York City." See Figure 4-1.

Specific deals vary, but the basic business model is to sell airtime across the company's fleet, with options that allow marketers to target specific areas or day parts.

Meanwhile, the company pays $80 to $125 per cab per month to the 350 cabs that currently run the ads.

That's a small fraction of the 12,187 cabs that currently serve the city, according to the *New York Times*. But each taxi-top billboard reaches 50,000 to 100,000 New Yorkers per day. The company is in

Figure 4-1. Adapt Media's taxi-top ad/runner service enables advertisers to target advertising based on a taxi's exact location. Photo: Adapt Media.

the process of expanding its operations, with one hundred cabs in Boston, seventy-five in Philadelphia, and fifteen in San Francisco.

"The amazing thing about these cabs is, they're extremely visible," says Christopher Young, vice president and advertising manager for J.P. Morgan Chase in Manhattan, which has signed a deal with Adapt for category exclusivity. The deal includes fifty dedicated cabs that run ads pointing out the company's 400 branches and 1,500 ATMs, 24/7. "People notice them. They get recognized."

Young says the ability to change messaging on the fly is particularly important to the company.

"We're optimizing usage versus just rotating messages," he says, "because of the fact that we use the GPS technology to transmit our nearest branch locations and rotate messages in language based on agreed-upon, preset neighborhoods."

The moment a cab turns onto Canal Street into Chinatown, the billboards instantly start posting messages in Mandarin. In parts of Queens with heavily Hispanic populations, the messages are posted in Spanish.

"A retail business like ours is dependent on getting people into our stores," says Young. "The unique ability to target your customer, to be able to actually direct them to the stores, is definitely revolutionary."

SERVING ADS IN A NEW YORK MINUTE

The patented media delivery system is a technological feat in itself. The ad|runner platform can deliver thousands of different ad campaigns to thousands of the individual taxi-top displays with a geographical accuracy of a few feet and a time accuracy of mere moments.

Advertisers access secure campaign management tools on the company's Web site to create their ads, and direct when and where they'd like them played. The system then sends the ads—complete with copy and some rudimentary graphics—wirelessly to the electronic panels for play out at the locations or times the advertiser has specified.

"People see relevant advertising appear right in front of them," says Katz. "And unlike advertising on cell phones, there are no privacy issues."

If a cab loses a connection with the system, or is on a break, it will automatically resume its programming once a new connection is made.

Best of all, advertisers can update taxi-top messages with new promotions or announcements within moments, and they receive performance reports and billing information over the Web, including the actual display times, duration, and locations their ads ran.

"You have to understand, waiting for a street light is productivity time in this town," says Time Warner's Novet. "I've seen people on the street corner going, 'Wow, look at that, the weather report, or the sports scores, or that sale.'"

"It's about delivering the right message at the right time at the right location," says Katz. "It's changing the way people think about getting information from ads."

It's also just one way marketers are delivering targeted advertising in the emerging wireless age.

WELCOME TO THE GREAT OUTDOORS

Take Smart Sign Media of Sacramento, California. Using sophisticated wireless sensing technology, the company operates roadside electronic billboards that continuously scan cars to detect which FM radio stations drivers are listening to—and then serve up advertising messages that best fit drivers' demographic profiles.

"Most people don't realize that when you're listening to a radio station, the antenna on your car picks up the frequency from the transceiver, and there's some leakage that then seeps out of the antenna," explains company CEO Tom Langeland. "Sensors on our signs measure the leakage frequency that comes off the antenna of each car that drives by. The technology can differentiate between one car and the next" up to one hundred cars per second. "It doesn't pick up the same [signal] twice."

If the freeway is packed with classical music listeners, drivers are more likely to see an ad for a luxury car or a high-end retailer. If hip-hop is tops, the billboard might change to athletic shoes or an upcoming movie.

The sensors, specially equipped dishes from Phoenix-based solutions provider Moiré, collect the frequency information from each car. The data is then aggregated, providing a ranking of which radio stations cars are tuned to. The technology matches the aggregate data to demographic profiles of people who listen to the detected radio stations using statistical data from Houston-based research firm The Media Audit. Armed with that information, the billboard is programmed to serve up the most targeted advertisement for the demographic makeup of the people expected to see the sign at any given hour.

"The Media Audit data provides information about how much money this group of drivers make on average, how many pets they have, whether they shop at Raley's or Ralph's, how many vacations they take, whether they are gamblers—you name it," says Langeland.

According to the *New York Times*, Smart Sign client Future Ford, a car-and-truck dealership off I-80 in Roseville, California, knows that on weekdays, drivers on that stretch of freeway tend to tune into a country music station, while evenings find drivers who are more apt to listen to talk radio and adult contemporary. So the dealership advertises for the Ford F-150 during the day, and Tauruses and Escorts in the evening.[1]

Langeland says another sign helped a Nissan dealer in San Leandro, California, custom-tailor advertisements to prospects as they drove by. "The dealer was really excited because he knew he was putting up the most highly sought-after offer" at any given time, says Langeland.

Today, the company operates fifteen signs scattered around Los Angeles, Sacramento, San Francisco, and Dallas. Each of the signs is connected to Smart Sign headquarters via the Web. This enables the company to serve up the ads digitally to any of the billboards, where they are cached and displayed during the part of the day that best fits each client's needs.

"This is the first time anyone's matched real-time data with outdoor advertising," says Langeland. "This is proving to be a highly efficient way to reach targeted consumers with the most compelling messages possible." See Figure 4-2.

Smart Sign may be on to something. While consumers scowl at television commercials, and go apoplectic over pop-up advertising, they appear to be quite receptive to sales pitches on the open

Figure 4-2. Electronic signs from Smart Sign Media use wireless technology to sense the radio stations drivers listen to, and then serve up advertisements that best fit drivers' demographic profiles. Photo: Smart Sign Media.

road. A recent study by marketing research firm Arbitron, for instance, found that nearly 30 percent of consumers said a billboard or other roadside message has led them to visit a retail store within a week of seeing the ad.[2]

Of course, all this talk of monitoring consumers' listening habits does sound a wee bit Orwellian.

But Langeland says the privacy-conscious can relax. "Yes, I would say it's an invasion of privacy if I knew who you were," he says. Since the system aggregates the data, "You're an 'it.' You're a number in the crowd. There's no way to tie you back to a database."

Indeed, state governments and industry trade group the Traffic Audit Bureau have long collected data on drivers' exposure to billboards, drawing rubber hoses across highways to count cars. It's all just statistical data that poses no threat to drivers' privacy, but can have a huge impact on marketers.

While early versions of the smart sign technology sample passing radios and then calculate the listening patterns of drivers so ads can be matched to the time of day, newer versions promise to serve up ads the instant the demographic makeup of drivers matches advertisers' desired target profiles.

Citing the need for accountability in today's fragmented media world, Langeland says the same technology can also help retailers understand their customer base, and better target other kinds of media buys.

"We can actually put the [tracking device] in your parking lot to measure exactly who your clients are" based on their radio listening habits, he says, so clients can better choose where to place radio advertising, for instance.

"These Arbitron studies and Scarborough studies are usually six months old by the time they get out, and their sample sizes—and accuracy—are highly questionable," he adds, referring to the predominant radio ratings tracking firms that typically rely on written diaries to monitor radio consumption. By contrast, "we technically survey thousands and thousands with passive surveys every day. It doesn't require any thinking, and it doesn't require any interaction with the person being surveyed. With that kind of data, you can pick and choose when to advertise, and which radio stations you need to be on."

NIELSEN TO GO

Wireless technology is even turning Smart Sign's strategy on its head in order to track consumer exposure to billboards, bus shelters, and taxi-top displays throughout the entire day.

Ratings services for television, radio, and Web-based marketing have long been able to pinpoint, say, how many eighteen- to thirty-four-year-old women click on an ad for Almay 16-Hour Mascara, or how many prepubescent boys will catch a spot for "Wurmz & Dirt" gross-out candy. But aside from nascent efforts like Smart Sign, the $2.65 billion-a-year outdoor advertising world has never been fully able to deliver reliable information on who's seeing which billboards and when.[3] As a result, outdoor's share of advertising spending has been a fraction of that of network television, which tops $21.22 billion a year.

To narrow the gap, television rating firm Nielsen Media Research has quietly launched Nielsen Outdoor, a new service that is using GPS technologies to track consumers while they're driving. Think Nielsen Families for the Fast Lane.

"Outdoor advertising is what we call 'the last of the great unmeasured media,'" says Lorraine Hadfield, managing director of the organization. "There really has been no empirical way to measure outdoor in the past."

After all, as Smart Sign's Langeland indicated, systems that ask people to keep a diary or recall where they've traveled are iffy at best. And knowing how many cars pass a billboard tells you little about how many people are in the car, who they are, how often they're exposed to the ad, and whether they actually notice it. But wireless technology changes all that.

In 2005, Nielsen Outdoor began rolling out a service that uses a small, cell phone–size device that uses GPS and proprietary software to provide highly accurate reach and frequency data for out-door advertisements, complete with demographics.

As John Connolly, a thirty-year outdoor ad veteran and VP of out-of-home media buying agency MedicaCom, put it to *Advertising Age*: "This is the most revolutionary development in outdoor since I've been in the industry."[4]

During early tests for the service in the Chicago area, Hadfield recruited 750 volunteers who agreed to carry the device, called the Npod, or Nielsen Personal Outdoor Device, everywhere they went for ten days.

"We knew that people are exposed to outdoor advertising irre-spective of the mode of travel, whether on foot, the bus, the train, or whatever," says Hadfield, "We knew we had to develop a per-sonal, wireless device that people could carry about the size of the smallest cell phone."

Participants, prescreened to establish demographic profiles, al-lowed their every movement to be tracked and recorded. Every twenty seconds, the Npod captured each user's latitude and longi-tude, while a computer system compared the data with the coordi-nates of 12,000 "geo-coded" outdoor sites in the Chicago region, including bus shelters, standard posters, billboards, and overhead signs.

SUDDEN IMPACT

To establish the user's likely exposures to an outdoor advertise-ment, the system applied a mind-boggling number of variables—including driver speed, the angle of the display to the road, its distance from the curb, the distance from which the display is first visible, the height of the display, whether it's illuminated or ob-structed, and so on—as users enter "impact zones," or the point of impression.

Nielsen knows, for instance, that three-quarters of the people who travel under a 200-square-foot sign above a highway overpass actually look at it, while only 30 percent of those who drive past a bus shelter actually see it.[5]

The data is then compared to demographics from each user to give a very accurate view of the reach and frequency of an outdoor ad campaign. Findings from that Chicago study dispelled one enduring myth about outdoor advertising. More than 50 percent of all outdoor advertising impressions among Chicago-area residents earning more than $100,000 a year occurred in low-income neighborhoods—contradicting the long-standing view that only the location of outdoor sites determines who is exposed to an ad message.[6]

All of this is factored into reports that assign "ratings" to all the outdoor sites in the area, enabling media buyers to manage outdoor ad spending as never before possible.

New York City is next to come on board, followed by eight other markets, including Los Angeles, Philadelphia, and the San Francisco–Oakland–San Jose area.

"Now we can tell you not just how many people saw a sign, but exactly how many and who they are," says Hadfield. "You know the age, the sex, the income, and how many times they are exposed to the ad."

All of which will come in handy as marketers increasingly turn their sights to the wireless technologies that are opening up that most powerful place-based advertising vehicle of all: the automobile itself.

THE FAST AND THE CURIOUS

With several U.S. states considering or enacting laws limiting cell phone use in cars, automakers and technology providers are racing to develop the next generation of hands-free wireless technologies, embedded into our cars, to give drivers new ways to place calls, check e-mail, and even surf the Web—while driving.

Known within the industry as "telematics," these mostly voice-based technologies wirelessly connect vehicles to customized information and services—from roadside assistance to real-time traffic updates to stolen-vehicle tracking to alerting police in the event of a collision—all without consumers needing to futz with handsets.

"Hands-free calling is just the beginning," says industry analyst Rob Enderle. "If you start with hands-free phones, it's not a big step to move to other sorts of services."

Indeed, consumers are increasingly putting telematics on their new-car wish lists, as such features as GPS–based concierge services move down-market, from luxury cars to schlep-mobiles—from Lexus to Kia, and from Mercedes to Chevrolet. Already, 12 percent of all new U.S. automobiles feature telematics of some form, according to Telematics Research Group in Minnetonka, Minnesota. And according to Forrester Research, three-quarters of consumers are interested in receiving content on weather, directions, traffic, or road conditions in their cars.[7]

"We live in an increasingly connected world, and we want that connection extended to our cars," says Phil Magney, the research group's president and cofounder.

Fueled by the runaway success of General Motors's built-in On-Star system, such in-car connectivity is becoming a key selling point as drivers increasingly demand safety, productivity, and entertainment solutions while stuck in today's interminable traffic jams.

And with new and proposed U.S. legislation—along with already stringent laws in Japan, England, Italy, and elsewhere—29 million new vehicles are expected to feature some form of telematics by 2010, up substantially from 8.4 million in 2004, according to Magney.

As a result, the race is on—for service providers, auto manufacturers, and marketers alike.

NOT YOUR FATHER'S OLDSMOBILE

Launched a decade ago, General Motors leads automakers in telematics enrollment with its OnStar system.

With twenty-four-hour access to a human call center representative, OnStar boasts over 2.5 million subscribers who pay from

$16.95 a month for roadside assistance to $69.95 a month for a package that includes making event and restaurant reservations. And the company's Virtual Advisor service delivers news, sports, weather, location-based traffic information, and even stock quotes to drivers on the move.

Already available in fifty-one GM models, as well as cars from Lexus, Acura, Audi, and others, OnStar is on a roll. Its Virtual Advisor service is a big hit.

"We will [increasingly] look to our cars as a place where we can interact with these mobile technologies on a routine, part-of-our-life kind of basis," says Chet Huber, president of OnStar. "We're finding people are very interested in new services and . . . information that is relevant to them."[8]

No wonder competition looms large, as revenues from telematics products and services are estimated to reach $42 billion by 2010, up from nearly $1 billion in 1998, according to International Data Corporation.[9] As a result, an increasing number of "smart" cars are hitting the roadways.

Germany's Volkswagen's Golf eGeneration was the first mass-produced car with a live Internet connection. Featuring built-in consoles that integrate a Nokia mobile phone, content from MSN, and Internet access from Volkswagen subsidiary gedas, the car featured hands-free access to services ranging from weather, traffic conditions, e-mail, Internet banking, route planning, and Web surfing. Though the car was a bit ahead of its time, the company is exploring the use of built-in telematics in future cars as well.

"In most European countries, it is already prohibited to make telephone calls with a [handheld] cell phone," says Hans-Gerd Bode, a spokesperson for Volkswagen. "We see extraordinarily high potential for telematics."[10]

BMW offers GPS–based systems that alert European BMW owners to traffic developments along their routes and offer alternatives, as well as a new navigation system that finds parking lots at the driver's destination and indicates whether the lots have available parking spaces.

Meanwhile, an adaptor for many BMWs integrates with an Apple iPod so listeners can take their tunes on the road. The solution enables drivers to control their iPod through the vehicle's audio system.

"Look for more Internet connectivity in the future," predicts BMW spokesperson Dave Buchko, adding that his company is looking into applying Bluetooth technologies to offer integration with cell phones, PDAs, and other personal devices—without the need for docking stations.[11] "These technologies make the car a much more useful device."

Already, OnStar, DaimlerChrysler's Uconnect, upstarts like ATX and Cross Country Automotive, and even some wireless carriers deliver hands-free calling and real-time route guidance and directions to local merchants, as well as new m-commerce and communications capabilities.

For its part, Ford Motor Company has teamed up with Sprint PCS to launch the Mobile-Ease Hands-Free Communications System, which allows Bluetooth-enabled phones to seamlessly connect with Ford's in-car network. As a driver gets into the car, any ongoing or incoming calls to the driver's cell phone are seamlessly transferred to the vehicle's audio system to keep calls from being interrupted.

Ford is also working with the Minnesota Department of Transportation on testing one hundred high-tech cars that transmit traffic flow, congestion, and even the weather to a Condition Acquisition Reporting System (CARS) that aggregates data and reports it back to motorists to keep them out of harm's way. As these systems are built into future cars, they may become part of a feedback loop that transmits traffic conditions to other cars, or even to road signs for all motorists to see.

According to an early report from Forrester Research, possible future developments include commuter buddy lists that enable social or business conferences during evening commutes. And as telematics devices proliferate, telematics operators are beginning to aggregate the locations of millions of vehicles to offer real-time traffic updates that can reroute subscribers around congested roadways. But Forrester predicts that as an increasing number of commuters turn to these services to shorten commutes, the secondary routes will become just as crowded as the primary ones.

The result? Rather than simply providing the same routing information to all commuters, telematics operators could vary route guidance to reshape traffic patterns—and, conceivably, offer premium services that save the best routes for paying customers.[12]

DRIVERS WANTED

Hoping to steal business from automakers, aftermarket developers are speeding up launches of their own telematics offerings.

Companies such as Sirius Satellite Radio and XM Satellite Radio are just two telematics carriers who offer digital news, sports, music, and entertainment to 4 million subscribers. First introduced to consumers in 2001, XM and Sirius are custom-made to send shockwaves through the mind-numbing world of corporate-owned radio networks and their Britney-fied playlists of 200 songs in heavy—even oppressive—rotation.

"We like to say we make our music daily," says XM spokesperson Charles Robins. "We're talking a hundred living, breathing stations with a point of view."[13]

Indeed, XM and Sirius were conceived in the early 1990s as subscription-based alternatives to repetitive, commercial-laden local radio. Each of the companies quickly amassed over $1 billion in investment capital from the likes of General Motors, Clear Channel, Ford Motors, and DirectTV, among many others.

Today, XM operates from its headquarters in a converted printing plant in Washington, D.C., while Sirius works from its studios in midtown Manhattan.

Each company uses orbital satellites and a network of terrestrial repeaters in major cities to beam one hundred channels of all-digital music, talk, and sports programming to subscribers's satellite-ready receivers.

Subscribers of the services pay $12.95 a month to tune in to a decidedly eclectic mix of channels, including XM's Liquid Metal (think Pantera, Sepultura, Vampire Mooose, and other Top 40–

unfriendly bands) and Sirius's Area 63 (trance and progressive house music from Armin Van Burren, Agnelli & Nelson, and DJ Tiesto), to name just two.

In the future, these and other entrants could conceivably offer customized audio streams to front-seat passengers and streaming video and interactive gaming to backseat entertainment consoles.

But don't hold your breath, says Forrester Research's Magney. Even with 3G, cellular may be too slow to stream full movies. Instead, he foresees a day when these and other companies use Wi-Fi to quickly download movies to cars.

"Picture pulling into a convenience store or a gas station, and you go to a kiosk or even the gas pump and literally choose a movie or some other form of content, and it's downloaded wirelessly to the vehicle system while you fill the car with fuel," says Magney.

Already, the DMP2 home networking gadget from Tempe, Arizona–based Omnifi links up to your wireless home Wi-Fi network and then downloads the latest additions from your MP3 collection into your car.

And look for wireless carriers such as Verizon and Sprint PCS to increasingly turn to voice platforms from companies like Tellme Networks and BeVocal to create their own voice portals for delivering in-vehicle services, predicts Forrester Research.

In fact, telematics aren't just for the driving public. Take a company like DaimlerChrysler, which spends $3 billion a year on software downloads for hardware in its cars.[14] Just think how much they'd save if they could do it all wirelessly. And companies like UPS and FedEx increasingly use a wide array of telematics and handheld solutions—including cellular, GPS, Bluetooth, and Wi-Fi—to coordinate deliveries, to find directions, and to communicate with back-office systems.

Today, most such services are viewed as value-added features to enhance the brand experience for car manufacturers. In the future, they will be viewed as a key asset for gaining access to customers. And that access will enable entire ecosystems of services, up and down the value chain.

But that's not to say there aren't road hazards ahead.

READY TO ROLL?

Aside from standards for enabling telematics devices to communicate with one another across disparate wireless networks, there is ongoing debate about the efficacy and business sense of "pushed" advertising into cars.

OnStar offers directions and information about nearby restaurants, gas stations, local attractions, and services, but without paid inclusion.

"At this point, we believe that we want to stay as objective as we can in this process and follow the consumer's lead. So we have not set up any business relationships where we would preferentially slot a McDonald's over a Burger King over a Taco Bell," says Huber.

That's smart thinking. And even without push marketing, advertising of all sorts will evolve because of this new level of in-car connectivity. Today, 56 percent of drivers say a radio spot ad has led them to visit a store within a week of hearing it.[15] Thanks to the wireless Web, subscribers to future telematics services may even be able to opt in to receive targeted commercials based on their preferences.

"Say you're a big golf player," says Enderle. "Instead of hearing any old commercial for Palmolive, marketers could send you a commercial about the latest, greatest golf club. The opportunity is here to use this technology to make very effective offers and very effective ads."

In fact, says Enderle, this form of targeted advertising could subsidize the cost of the service for the subscriber. "You could say, 'Okay, I'm willing to listen to four or five ads on these days,' and what would otherwise cost $20 a month might come to you free."

And for the first time ever, drivers will be able to respond to radio commercials the instant they hear them. All at the touch of a button or a simple voice command.

Take Howard Stern. When the popular shock jock decided to move his show from broadcast radio syndication to the Sirius satellite radio system in 2006, it wasn't just because the FCC has been hounding him for indecency, or even just the estimated $500 million payday. It was because a direct and increasingly interactive line to the consumer means we're not just talking about the Howard Stern Show anymore. We're talking about the Howard Stern Shopping Network, where Howard can sell show paraphernalia, gear, clothing, books, and more. Not just from Stern and company, but even those products hawked by his guests and sponsors.

It was Stern and his merry band of mayhem makers, after all, who helped turn Snapple into a national brand worth $1.7 billion when it was sold to Quaker Oats a decade ago. Just think what he can do with a direct sales channel to his loyal fans.

Still, even without pushed advertising, wireless does come with a price.

In cases that have gained international attention, a Glendale, California, man was accused of secretly planting a GPS and cell phone device on his estranged girlfriend's car in order to track her every move.[16] And, quite legally, a Connecticut-based rental car company installed GPS into its vehicles to find stolen rental cars and charge customers for "dangerous" driving—including exceeding the posted speed limit. Without a warning on rental contracts, the company fined a customer $150 for each of three times he drove seventy-seven miles per hour.

"There are very legitimate issues that need to be very carefully controlled relative to the use of this kind of information," says OnStar's Huber.[17]

Then there's the same driver distraction that telematics were ostensibly designed to ameliorate. Despite technologies that enable activation of services by voice or minimal manual actions, the industry may be speeding toward what experts call "cognitive overload."

"Hands-free does not translate to risk-free," says Rae Tyson, a spokesman for the National Highway Traffic Safety Administration.

The NHTSA has conducted tests to measure distraction caused by manual- and voice-activated navigation systems, hand-free cell phones, and CD and DVD players, as well as eating, changing radio controls, applying makeup, and being engrossed in detailed conversations.

All of these activities have the potential to distract drivers at critical moments, and are estimated to account for 25 percent of all traffic accidents.

"Even if you have both hands on the wheel, you reach a point where even a detailed conversation can cause a safety issue," says Rae.

And as the number and sophistication of telematics devices grows—think about the "augmented reality" windshield we talked about earlier—so will the likelihood of laws limiting their use.

"Over the next few years, we're going to learn a lot about the nature of a whole assortment of hazards and whether they create significant liability for manufacturers," says Enderle. "That's going to dictate what this technology will mean moving forward."

Most in the industry agree, citing the issue as a motivating factor for finding new and inventive ways to make telematics devices even safer.

After all, you can't turn back the clock. People expect to communicate from their cars. So it's really a matter of the industry minimizing the distraction with safer and safer products.

Either way, one thing's for sure: From the unbound billboard to the wireless Winnebago, the commute home will never be the same—for commuters or the marketers who sell to them.

Photo: OnStar Corporation

Chet Huber:
Driving Ambition

As president of OnStar Corporation, Chet Huber has taken General Motors on a joy ride to the cutting edge of wireless technology.

A mild-mannered midwesterner from Hammond, Indiana, Huber first joined General Motors in 1972. After twenty-three years in a variety of engineering, operations, and marketing roles, Huber assumed the presidency of OnStar, a then little-known GM subsidiary.

Launched in 1995, OnStar combines cellular and GPS technologies to keep 2.5 million subscribers and their vehicles connected to human call center operators—and increasingly, the Internet—twenty-four hours a day. Over the last decade, OnStar has rolled out new services that enable subscribers to place mobile phone calls, hear news, sports, and soap opera updates, have their e-mail read to them, and even place stock transactions, at the press of a button.

Along the way, Huber has hit the ignition on an industry unlike anything that's ever hit the road.

RICK MATHIESON: What types of early telematic services are drivers gravitating toward most?

CHET HUBER: We continue to see significant interest in services for safety, security, and peace of mind. If an airbag deploys because the car has been in an accident, we'll call for help; if you press an emergency button because you've had an accident where the airbag didn't deploy, we'll respond.

We're helping to track 500 stolen vehicles a month. We're unlocking 35,000 doors a month for our customers across the United States and Canada. One of our services with tremendous future potential is our ability to interact with the car's electrical architecture in the area of diagnostics. Twenty-thousand times a month, customers call with some issue with car performance. We can actually perform vehicle triage for that customer and give them directions on what they should do next. We're also seeing in the neighborhood of 5.5 million calls a month being made using OnStar Personal Calling.

People are also very interested in news content, where they can get [news and sports] delivered to them on their morning drive in an audio fashion. And I can tell you, my daughter is really interested in one of the categories that is available in our Virtual Advisor service—namely soap opera updates. I can't go a day without having her push a button for her update on *One Life to Live.* Now I know the characters without ever having watched the program.

RM: The auto category is one of the largest marketing categories in the world. Beginning with Cadillac, you've begun creating differentiated services for individual automobile brands, versus one OnStar for all automobiles. How do services like these enhance the automotive brand experience?

CH: To a certain extent, we become the embedded customer relationship management [CRM] platform for the car manufacturer. We are literally one button press away from that customer being able to be in touch with someone who can handle everything from roadside assistance, all the way to being able to answer questions about a feature that might exist in that vehicle.

There's a tremendous opportunity to create a deep bond with the consumer, starting with provisioning a service that's really important to safety and security and ultimately extending into any of the relationships that have to do with the vehicle—scheduling subsequent maintenance, vehicle transactions, leases, even [preselling] the next vehicle. There are a number of ways that that relationship can be enhanced.

RM: GM has been a major force behind the development of XM Satellite Radio, which delivers content to drivers and their passengers on a subscription basis. What opportunities do services like these bring to marketers?

CH: We think it's a tremendous service opportunity in a convergence between satellite radio and a platform like OnStar. And we're managing the business toward that objective.

Today, satellite radio is kind of a one-way distribution into the vehicle. But that whole world could open up with a back channel that allows you to essentially interact with that content, or to facilitate purchases. A service like OnStar can act as the back channel in that kind of relationship.

Where vehicles might have an embedded navigation system, there's also an opportunity to populate pieces of that navigation system with real-time information that is relevant to the route someone is driving, whether that's to pop traffic incidents up on the navigation screen, or whatever else might be of interest. In the 2005 model year, we started to take a look at using XM Satellite bandwidth to interact with GM vehicles on navigation systems.

RM: That said, much fuss has been made about the idea of sending actual location-based advertising to drivers because consumers would find it too invasive. What's OnStar's position?

CH: In our minds, this will not cross a threshold, as some people have envisioned, where we're pushing information into the vehicle and essentially turning these technologies into verbal billboards where someone can scream out their store into your vehicle as you pass by. Everything that we are looking at from a privacy standpoint would tell us that that is probably a direction that doesn't make a lot of sense to go. We believe in following the consumer's lead, and [opt-in] marketing would seem, today at least, as the direction to go.

RM: OnStar does deliver messages about the next restaurant around the corner or nearest gas station, if the driver asks for it. Do sponsors get preferential listings?

CH: To this point, we have developed a supplier-agnostic information and recommendation position. We do provide connection to a rating-type service, and we provide information on restaurants and hotels based upon their classifications—two-star, three-star, and so on.

You would be amazed, but most of the time, our subscribers aren't just looking for the closest gas station. They want the closest Shell station or the closest Amoco station. They don't just want the closest hotel, they would like the closest Fairmont or the closest Holiday Inn or Sheraton. They don't generally tell you, "I need a cup of coffee. Can you tell me where coffee is?" They tell you, "Hey, where is the Starbucks?" or "Where is the Caribou Coffee?"

We have not set up any business relationships where we would preferentially slot a McDonald's over a Burger King over a Taco Bell. We have no preferential kind of treatment in our database today at all. A fairly fundamental decision that we felt we needed to make early was: At the end of the day, are we providing services to our customers, or are we brokering our subscriber base to third parties? Because of the nature of the relationship that we really aspired to have with our customers, we felt that the services have to be incredibly objective, without any of the kind of brokering aspect at all.

RM: Describe the world of telematics at the end of the decade.

CH: By 2010, the services that are the basis of what OnStar provides, this issue of being connected safe and secure while driving, will end up spanning all retail vehicles in the United States and Canada. And I think you're going to start to see them fundamentally changing the relationships people have with their vehicles.

There are numerous things that can happen when you think of a vehicle as an element on a high-speed, wireless data network. As technology allows faster and faster data rates between an off-board infrastructure and the vehicle, the potential exists for doing things like delivering rich entertainment data directly to the car; or software updates sent directly to the vehicle architecture. We'll have a tremendous ability to leverage, on an ongoing basis, the vehicle's infrastructure and the location component to come up with some pretty interesting new services. But I also think it's a safe bet that the highest-used services of tomorrow are the ones we couldn't even dream of today.

CHAPTER FIVE

The Wireless Point of Persuasion

Shopping for Insights at the Store of the Future

Germany's Metro AG has a message to the world: Retailing's wireless future is open for business, today.

The company's Extra Future Store is a high-tech supermarket that features wireless checkout, "smart shelves" that alert staff to product shortages, and a "VeggieVision" produce scale that sorts grapefruit and cantaloupe using a digital camera.

"This is the first time that you find almost all modern IT systems for retailing integrated into one place," says Albrecht von Truchsess, a spokesperson for Düsseldorf-based Metro AG, the world's third-largest supermarket chain.

Metro has quietly teamed with over forty partners, including SAP, Intel, IBM, and Procter & Gamble, in an ambitious effort to gain insights into how supermarkets can use advanced wireless technologies to cut costs and attract customers in the decade ahead. And it's proving that wireless is far more than just fun and games via consumer cell phones. It's proving that wireless technologies play an integral part of what have become known as intelligent, connected retail environments.

During Extra's first year of operations, over 15,000 shoppers—and 13,000 international observers—have trekked to this 4,000-

square-foot store in the tiny town of Rheinberg to experience the supermarket of tomorrow.

"The idea is to see how customers react, what technologies they accept, and what they don't like," says von Truchsess. "If it works here in Rheinberg, it can work in other places, too."

Among Extra's high-tech features:

▶ Grocery carts are equipped with wireless touch-screen "personal shopping assistants" that provide information on products and where to find them. The assistants also provide an easy link to personal grocery lists. Shoppers use a Web site to make out their list, and then call them up via the assistant when they get to the store. See Figure 5-1.

"Your wife can make a shopping list at home, and if you stop off on the way home from work, you can access the list from the shopping assistant," says von Truchsess.

▶ A wireless self-scanning system enables customers to scan the bar codes from grocery items directly into the shopping assistant, which then transmits the total to the checkout stand. Nearly 10,000 customers—one-third of Rheinberg's residents—have signed up for special loyalty cards that they swipe to activate self-scanning and to receive promotional offers.

▶ VeggieVision, a so-called smart scale, outfitted with a tiny camera, instantly identifies the fruit or vegetable being weighed, and then prints out the appropriate price sticker.

▶ Kiosks serve up information about food items, and even play video and audio clips from DVDs and CDs.

Figure 5-1. At the Extra Future Store in Rheinberg, Germany, "personal shopping assistants" help shoppers organize their shopping, and enable wireless self-scanning for faster checkouts. Photo: METRO Group.

"You can pick up a bottle of wine, hold it against the scanner on the kiosk, and get information on the wine, a video of the region it comes from, and recipes for meals that go with that wine," says von Truchsess.

If you can't find a grocery item, the kiosk will activate small light beams in the floor that direct you to the product.

▶ Electronic shelf labeling and advertising displays give store managers the ability to wirelessly update product prices and promotions from a central merchandise management system, mapping supply with demand in real time.

Meanwhile, extensive use of radio frequency identification (RFID) technology keeps the store's supply chain operations humming, while freeing up staff to attend to customers.

RFID–based "smart tags"—those tiny silicon chips that store product data and use a miniature antenna to wirelessly communicate with networks—are attached to pallet loads of products being shipped to the store from distribution centers.

With smart tags, electronic "readers" mounted on dock doors at distribution centers and store stockrooms "interrogate" the tags and instantly transmit quantities and other product information to managers without the need for manual counting.

A number of so-called smart shelves extend RFID into the store, using shelf-mounted readers along with tags on over 37,000 individual items to alert personnel if stocks are running low, or if expiration dates are approaching for supplies of everything from cream cheese to chocolate milk.

"One of the biggest benefits of RFID is the synergies not just in the supply chain, but throughout the store," says Erik Michielsen, director of RFID and ubiquitous technologies for ABI Research in Oyster Bay, New York. "[It can] provide consumers substantial benefits through better product availability, and potentially lower costs, due to increased efficiencies."

"This technology could radically change the relationship between the customer and the product," says retail technology expert James Crawford. "Fast-forward ten years, and it could change the paradigm of what retailing is all about."[1]

RADAR LOVE

Indeed, one day, the postage-sized tags could be on everything—cars, books, beverages, wristwatches, credit cards—enabling items to wirelessly connect to networks or the Internet.

Using electronic product code identification technology, called "ePC," smart tags use radio signals to communicate with computers or even home appliances and connect them to information, instructions, or identification via the Web. The devices could then use the information to provide whole new forms of product innovations.

Imagine a Gucci blouse that tells the washing machine, "Don't wash me, I'm dry clean only." Medicines that warn users of dangerous interactions. Ice cream containers that adjust the temperature in the freezer for optimal storage. Or coffee machines that serve up the best brew based on the type of bean being used. See Figure 5-2.

"The goal is to design and implement standards that connect physical products to the virtual world," says Dan Engels, a researcher who has worked with retail giant Wal-Mart to conduct tests of the technology as part of an MIT–sponsored research program. "There are literally hundreds of applications that can benefit from products that communicate with the virtual world."[2]

"It essentially turns the next-generation Internet into a 'Thingernet,'" says Tim Kindberg, a researcher at HP Labs, which is developing a host of RFID technologies.[3]

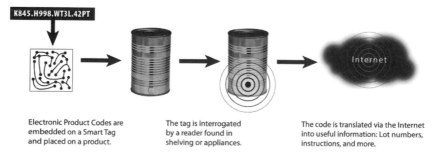

K845.H998.WT3L.42PT

Electronic Product Codes are embedded on a Smart Tag and placed on a product.

The tag is interrogated by a reader found in shelving or appliances.

The code is translated via the Internet into useful information: Lot numbers, instructions, and more.

Figure 5-2. "Smart tag" technology enables products to communicate with home appliances or the Web, heralding an era of "intelligent products." Image: Sarah Khorey, based on information from the Auto-ID Center.

Today, the technical complexity of many of these scenarios is wildly prohibitive. And the legal ramifications of value propositions involving product warnings or instructions must still be worked out.

But that's not stopping companies like Wal-Mart, Procter and Gamble, Kraft, and many other category-leading companies from spending nearly $1.9 billion a year on RFID and other forms of wireless technology—a figure that could top $3 billion by 2009— in efforts to create the ultimate in "experiential branding," they may end up transforming the way customers interact with stores and even individual products.[4, 5]

FOOD ON THE MCFASTRAK

McDonald's Corporation—the world's largest restaurant chain— has conducted tests with Southern California's Transportation Corridor Agency on wireless electronic-payment systems that allow drive-through customers to pay for their Big Mac and fries via FasTrak transponders, the ubiquitous badges affixed to millions of California cars to pay for toll roads.

Here's how it works. Antennas stationed in drive-through lanes of four of McDonald's Orange County locations read radio signals sent by the transponders. Once an order is placed, drivers pay by cash or have their meals billed to their FasTrak account, just the way they pay for toll roads.

Over 15,000 California drivers used the service during a three-month trial, and a similar system was tested at 400 Chicago-area McDonald's locations, enabling customers to place purchases using their ExxonMobil SpeedPass key fob. Early results indicated consumers focused less on price and more on the food, often increasing the average order size. Best of all, the actual transaction process was accelerated and more accurate because everything was handled electronically.

The effort is part of a transition toward what McDonald's calls a national cashless initiative aimed at increasing consumer convenience. Using a standards-based infrastructure, the company is rolling out cashless transaction capabilities to 8,000 restaurants nationwide, with more to come. Today, this mostly means enabling credit and debit cards at sales terminals. But the infrastructure makes it easy to deploy wireless payments as consumer demand increases.

"Our solution is flexible enough to address anything that can be connected to it," says Stan Washington, director of technology for the Western division of McDonald's Corporation in San Diego, California. "The possibilities with wireless are endless . . . the only thing that would stop us is our own lack of imagination."

I'll say. Anyone who spends as much time as I do on San Francisco Bay Area freeways and bridges is, by now, a FasTrak fanatic. When it comes to 134 million trips they make over Bay Area bridges each year, morning commuters know the drive can go one of two ways. A living hell of interminable waiting times to throw $3 of your hard-earned cash at a disgruntled tollbooth operator. Or a mad dash (sometimes a demolition derby) to merge into the Fas-Trak lane, zoom through the terminal, and get on your merry way as fast as your wheels and the caffeine kick from your morning coffee will carry you.

I also happen to have an irrational obsession with the Golden Arches. In the firmament of drive-time 'fast food, Mayor McCheese is my copilot. And if I'm any indication, a combo meal of RFID and French fries could drive my beloved Mickey D's into some super-size profits. But FasTrak is far from the only option out there for marketers and consumers alike.

Today, over 6 million consumers use ExxonMobil's popular SpeedPass badges—devices based on the same technology FasTrak uses—allowing them to pull up to the pump, wave a little wand on their key chain near an RFID reader built into the pump, and start filling up—with payment made instantaneously. Stop & Shop stores use the same technology to enable customers to pick up groceries and sundry items and just wave key or wristwatch fobs and walk out the door.

Two NFL teams recently deployed RFID readers at point-of-sale terminals scattered throughout their home stadiums. The Seattle

Seahawks' Qwest Field, for instance, has installed fifty-six "Power-Pay" readers, while the Philadelphia Lincoln Financial Field has deployed readers at all 401 of its point-of-sale terminals. Using their ExxonMobil SpeedPass fobs, customers can pay for food, drinks, and memorabilia. During trials, the stadiums found transaction time was twice as fast as cash, and almost six times faster than a credit or debit card. Better yet: Customers spent twice as much money with the system than with either cash or credit cards.[6]

LOST IN SPACE

Despite its impact on the shopping experience, most of the attention on RFID today is based on inventory management. This may seem like a rather prosaic use of a technology that packs such punch, except when you consider that smart shelves like those at the Extra Future Store mean that stores are better able to predict demand and ensure that consumers can always find what they're looking for.

Studies conducted by Gillette indicate that shoppers typically find that 8 percent of what they're looking for is out of stock on any typical weekday, climbing to 11 percent on Sunday.[7]

"Our number one reason for participating in the test is to see how we can improve the availability of our products at retail," says Gillette spokesperson Steve Breighten.[8]

The problem: "slippage"—theft or loss of product, whether in-transit or in-store.

Remarkably, Gillette, which was recently acquired by P&G, experiences some of the industry's highest theft rates—up to 20 percent of its razors are stolen in retail stores worldwide, according to industry expert Jeffrey Jacobsen, former CEO of RFID chip manufacturer Alien Technologies.[9]

Unfortunately, today's antitheft devices are only about 20 percent effective; thieves can handle the transponder so readers can't see the items they're stealing.[10]

"Typically, someone buys razors in two to three packages at a time," says Gillette's Breighten. "Smart tags could send a signal that a large number of packages have been taken off the shelf at one time, which means there's probably a theft in progress."

In another test, Home Depot, which prides itself on hiring licensed contractors as in-store service personnel—found that its staff spends 75 percent of its time checking shelves and only 25 percent of time helping customers.[11]

By using smart tags and handheld readers to count inventory, the company discovered it could effectively reverse those percentages—freeing staff to attend to customer service.

The Gap is also using RFID. The San Francisco–based company has been conducting field tests with smart shelves that alert store staff when any item is out of stock so it can be replenished immediately.[12]

"The primary component of RFID is to ensure that inventory is well ordered, well organized, and available to customers," says ABI's Michielsen. "For a company like the Gap, it means that the 36-waist, 34-length jeans are on the right shelf so customers find what they want. And the store doesn't miss any sales because of an unstocked shelf, or because they didn't know they have supplies in the backroom."

Indeed, this ability to alert clerks when backroom or in-store stocks run low—by theft or otherwise—may be the single most important motivating factor for adopting the technology over the near term.

"We want a real-time demand signal to add value to consumers and take costs out of the supply chain," says Larry Kellam, director of supply chain innovation for Procter & Gamble.[13] According to Kellam, the company hopes that such replenishment alerts will save the company up to $1.6 billion a year in supply chain costs.[14]

But RFID certainly isn't the only wireless technology behind the intelligent, connected retail environments of tomorrow.

WORTH YOUR AISLE

In addition to testing a variation on Extra's Shopping Assistant, called a Shopping Buddy, Stop & Shop markets is also testing the

Everywhere Display, a new "pervasive" computing solution from IBM.

Beamed from the supermarket ceiling, this solution transforms any surface, like, say, the grocery aisle floor, into an interactive display.

For example, say you're in the packaged meals aisle, and you have specific dietary needs or would like some information on the health benefits of fiber relative to the products around you. You can tap on the projected display with your foot and view information on the "screen." The system will even point you to the product it thinks will give you the most sawdust per serving.

At this writing, the solution is only deployed in a handful of stores. But if tests go well, the Everywhere Displays could be rolled out at over 150 Stop & Shop locations.[15]

Meanwhile, a study from Gartner Group indicates that 31 percent of retailers are installing or considering wireless point-of-sale devices or wireless checkout solutions over the next few years.[16]

Most new systems will involve swiping a credit card. Others may use RFID. The Gap, for instance, is exploring the use of RFID to enable mass scanning at checkout and instantly processing returns, loss prevention, and loyalty discounts.[17]

"Most big retail companies right now say that [wireless check out] is out of scope; we're going to do the supply chain stuff first," says Elgar Fleisch, a professor at the University of Gallen's Institute of Technology Management and cochair of Auto-ID Labs, a federation of research universities developing the foundation for intelligent, connected products and environments—an "Internet of things," in industry parlance. "But to be honest, all of them know they would save the most money by automating checkout."

According to Fleisch, the ability to walk into a store, throw goods in your bag, and walk out without writing a check, digging for cash, or swiping a credit card, is about ten to fifteen years away.

In the meantime, more rudimentary point-of-sale solutions like those from NCR and m-Qube, as well as others from Fujitsu, enable supermarkets and other stores to integrate with, say, their loyalty card programs to deliver coupons and other marketing messages to consumers who opt in to receive offers via their handsets or specially rigged shopping carts as they stroll through the store. Re-demption at checkout closes the loop and provides convenience for all involved.

For a system like Fujitsu's "U-Scan Shopper," which calls up video offers based on an individual shopper's location within the store, a typical retailer might spend between $100,000 to $150,000 for carts, servers, interrogator beacons, and database systems, according to estimates from *eWeek*.[18]

"That's part of the value of mobile," says Jim Manis, m-Qube's vice president of industry development. "It's so pervasive, you can begin to take advantage of intelligent databases so that as customers ask for data, you can actually supply it to them, right then and there."

Beyond transactions, other immersive technologies are enabling ever more novel capabilities for creating breakthrough in-store promotions.

YOU WON'T BELIEVE YOUR EARS

Companies from McDonald's to Procter & Gamble are experimenting with new technology that can pick you out of a crowd and deliver audio content so only you can hear it. Not merely in your ears, mind you. In your head.

Called "targeted audio," these new technologies direct sound much as a laser beam directs light. Sound waves are converted to an ultrasonic beam, or even spherical sound "bubbles," that can be directed to specific objects or individuals in its path.

Point the beam at a wall, and the sound will come from that wall. Step into the beam, and sounds are converted into audible frequencies that are so targeted, they seem to materialize from within your own skull.

"There's a real 'wow factor,'" says Suzanne Kantra, an editor for *Popular Science* who has evaluated the technology. "If you disrupt the beam, the sound is generated where you're standing, and it seems like it's coming from within your own head."[19]

A slight alteration in the direction of the beam can cause the audio to rove around from ear to ear, for the ultimate in surround sound. You hear a sonata, a news flash, or a product pitch. The person standing next to you doesn't hear a thing.

"The sound can be projected in a very narrow beam, much like a visual spotlight," says Dr. Frank Joseph Pompei, a former MIT Labs researcher with a master's degree in psychoacoustics.

His firm, Watertown, Massachusetts–based Holosonic Research Labs, Inc., produces the Audio Spotlight, one of only a few targeted audio devices on the market.

"You can point sound at one person, and they're the only ones who can hear it," he says.

"It's a lot like wearing headphones—only without messing up your hair," adds Elwood G. Norris, chairman of San Diego–based American Technology Corporation, which produces a rival product called the HyperSonic Sound (HSS) system.

According to Pompei, DaimlerChrysler and General Motors are planning to outfit new cars with Holosonic's Audio Spotlights. There are four in Chrysler's MAXXcab concept truck, for instance. "[There's] one over each seating position in the car, so each occupant can choose his own music," says Pompei. But it's the technology's laser-sharp targeting capability, which can create sound beams as small as five to six inches in diameter, that could transform the way we experience audio content.

Imagine a music store where Little Joey can sample the Black Eyed Peas' "Hey Mama" at full blast, while Mom croons to the soothing sounds of Norah Jones's "Sunrise," just two feet away.

Imagine a sports bar with ten or fifteen televisions set to football, soccer, basketball, and boxing. At your table, you can choose which ones you want to hear, and the sound is beamed right to you—while the group at the next table listens to something else.

Imagine nightclubs where dance floors feature different musical zones—say Disco, Techno, Hip-Hop, and Salsa—with none of them overlapping.

Or imagine extremely targeted message bubbles in every aisle of the grocery store, each with an audio commercial pitching everything from ginkgo biloba dietary supplements to Depends undergarments. See Figure 5-3.

And just think of the twisted things that targeted audio could do in the hands of the perfidious pranksters at MTV's *Punk'd*. ("Did you hear that voice?" "Um, no.")

Both Norris and Pompei admit hearing from folks who are alarmed by the notion of commercial messages being beamed to their heads.

"It's a headphone effect," says Norris, laughing. "It's not like it's invading someone's mind."

And it's an effect that's getting a lot of notice in retail circles. *Popular Science* recently awarded Norris's HyperSonic Sound a "Best of What's New" award for general electronic inventions. And marketers at McDonald's, Coca-Cola, and several major museums are evaluating or deploying the technology to beam product enticements from point-of-purchase displays.

According to Norris, the largest McDonald's in the world, a 1,000-seat location at The Smithsonian Institute's National Air & Space Museum, is testing targeted audio just so counter staff can hear orders above the restaurant's cacophonous ambient noise. The store is even using the technology to beam special offers to customers.

"If the manager finds out he's got a large supply of chicken nuggets he wants to push, he can run an instantaneous special and alert customers," says Norris. "It's multilingual, so if you stand in line, you'll hear a special offer in English or Spanish."

"There are so many possible applications," says *Popular Science*'s Kantra. "It's the most promising audio advance in years."[20]

Figure 5-3. Targeted audio technology can deliver audio content that seems to emanate from within your own head. Image: American Technology Corporation.

FROM PRADA, WITH LOVE

As I mentioned earlier, some of the most compelling applications of these and other technologies is occurring at upscale Prada, a kind of Mecca to fashionistas the world over.

At Prada's "Epicenter" stores in New York and Los Angeles, sales associates use Wi-Fi–based tablet PCs to scan RFID tags on clothes—the tags are clear so you can see the chip and antenna—to check inventories or to make recommendations based on past purchase behavior. Does that $2,200 suit come in your size? What colors is it available in? The answers are always at your fingertips. Associates can even use the devices as remote controls, calling up videos of runway models adorned in the garment via displays around the store.

"A large portion of Prada's business comes from a very small subset of shoppers," says Rachael McBrearty, vice president of creative strategy for technology consulting firm IconNicholson, which deployed the technology for Prada. "This is one way to provide very personalized experience and develop a relationship with top customers."

As shoppers make their way around the store, or place items on tables or chairs for later consideration, readers embedded in furniture scan the tag and automatically display the associated runway video, designer sketches, or information about the availability, cut, color, fabric, and other materials used in the garment on the nearest display. The content can also be linked to the sales associates' tablets so they know what items shoppers are carrying around.

In the dressing rooms, shoppers can access much of this same content on an interactive touch screen display. When in default mode, the display plays video—dubbed "aura"—that is usually built around content associated with the selected clothing collection, including the images and inspirations that led to its design. And while each shopper tries on the clothes, the dressing room's "Magic Mirror" takes time-delay video and replays the action in slow motion so the shopper can take in the full effect.

Opened for business in 2001, the first Epicenter store, in New York, was launched in an effort by Miuccia Prada and her husband, CEO Patrizio Bertelli, to bring fresh energy to the brand. Bertelli, the consummate businessman and passionate America's Cup yachts-man, focused on the technology—much of it wireless—to create competitive differentiation. And he succeeded spectacularly.

"Prada really likes to be cutting-edge, whether it's in yacht rac-ing or in their clothing designs—that's what their brand is all about," says McBrearty. "They wanted to be leaders in creating a whole new shopping experience."

Designed by famed Dutch architect Rem Koolhaas and nearly two dozen engineering, technology, and design firms, the store cost, by some estimates, upward of $40 million.[21] It gained instant recognition as a technological marvel. But it wasn't without diffi-culties.

The store opened just a few months after the 9-11 terrorist at-tacks, and on the cusp of what turned out to be a protracted eco-nomic downturn. And the New York store has been buffeted by an assortment of business issues—some of them tied to the tech-nology.

Maintaining the technological infrastructure, for instance, was no small feat. Some of the technology wasn't intuitive enough for customers. And sales associates were sometimes slow to take up the new sales tools. Of course, they don't call it the cutting edge for nothing—and the Epicenter store is viewed by all involved as one-part concept store, one-part laboratory for discovering what customers will embrace or dismiss in the retail experience.

"Prada is motivated to impact the brand and experiment a bit to see how to use technology to move its brand forward," says Tom Nicholson, managing director for IconNicholson. "Some things will work, and others won't—either way, Prada will be at the fore-front."

Indeed, the luxury retailer is applying lessons learned from its early implementation for a next generation of innovations, as well as an emphasis on training.

"One of the things we learned early on was that there are limits to the technology, and sometimes it's better to train the sales asso-ciates than it is to expect customers to be able to adapt to it," says McBrearty. She adds that the company now makes sure sales asso-ciates are trained to use the technology as a tool, because, as she puts it, "You don't want to have a customer frustrated by the tech-nology when it's there to serve them."

What's more, the original devices deployed for sales associates—bulky PDAs with huge battery packs—have been replaced by more functional and streamlined tablets. Older RFID tags that required very close proximity to readers have been updated. And the entire infrastructure is being streamlined for easier maintenance.

"The technology just gets cooler by the day," says McBrearty. "It really is the future of retailing."

And more and more brands are discovering its virtues.

TAG, YOU'RE IT

Up-and-coming couture brand Nanette Lepore is experimenting with what's called the Lepore Looking Glass, in-store mirrors that interact with on-clothing RFID tags at the company's SoHo store. Hold a houndstooth suit or a Persian Lamb jacket and chiffon skirt ensemble up to the mirror, and a transparent video monitor housed within the mirror's glass reveals itself to play animated scenarios featuring the brand's whimsical Lepore Girl mascot upselling accessories and complementary items.

And Barnes & Noble is exploring the idea of binding RFID tags on books and magazines and embedding readers around stores to activate touch-screen messages—sales promotions or other special offers—based on the merchandise that customers have in hand as they stroll around the store.

It all gets even more ingenious when you look at RFID's ability to offer insights into consumer buying behavior. ACNielsen is one of a handful of companies hoping to help companies mine data collection enabled by RFID to unlock insights into customer purchases at the point where many decisions are made—in the store itself. For instance, ACNielsen could use the tags to measure "in-store behaviors such as browsing, indecision, or direct product comparisons," Ted Fichuk, the company's senior vice president, writes in a company trends report.[22] For the first time ever, stores can measure things such as products that are picked up and then returned to the shelf—representing what Fichuk calls "a great leap in understanding consumer choice . . . completely altering promotional decisions."

Still, for all the attention these and other scenarios receive, it's RFID's less glamorous role for a certain other retailer that will transform twenty-first-century retailing.

That's because Linda Dillman, Wal-Mart's chief information officer, has mandated that the retailer's top 300 suppliers adopt RFID for supply chain management applications by 2006, with the rest on board by the end of the decade.

"RFID represents the marriage of logistics and information technology that gives us a superior way to track our inventories and manage them," says Tom Williams, a spokesperson for the Bentonville, Arkansas–based company. "We think we do our supply chain management very well already. But RFID brings to the forefront so many more efficiencies."[23]

Indeed, Extra, Stop & Shop, and Prada's deployments notwithstanding, Wal-Mart's move represents the technology's most powerful endorsement yet.

"Nobody's taken such a gigantic leap forward in RFID," says Williams.

With over 4,800 stores around the globe, Wal-Mart is the world's largest retailer. And it was Wal-Mart's backing of the bar code in the 1970s that provided the heft needed to make that more primitive technology an industry standard for keeping track of inventories.

"Wal-Mart will galvanize the industry toward RFID adoption," says Forrester analyst Christine Overby. "It's like the E.F. Hutton of old: When Wal-Mart speaks, people listen."[24]

But as some retailers are quickly finding out, that influence is not without controversy.

SMART SHELVES, DUMB PROBLEMS

While many retailers are already extending RFID from the stockroom to the storefront, Wal-Mart, for one, postponed plans to bring the technology to store shelves at its Brockton, Massachusetts site.[25]

The Electronic Privacy Information Center, Consumers Against Supermarket Privacy Invasion and Numbering, and other privacy groups have been blasting Wal-Mart's smart shelf plans for fear that RFID tags placed on individual items could one day lead to Big Brother–like monitoring of consumer behavior.

"That's just not going to happen," responds industry expert Sanjay Sarma, a former chairman of research for the Auto–ID Center, a predecessor to the Auto–ID Labs.[25]

That's because readers and tags can only speak to each other over a very short distance, and cannot work through certain materials.

"The idea of someone driving by in a van to read the stuff in your medicine cabinet, that's really just impossible," he says.

To firmly address the brouhaha, industry advocates have called for "kill switches" in smart tags, so consumers can opt out of any postpurchase features built into the technology.

"We have a very clear privacy policy based on two tenets. One is choice, and the other is awareness," says Sarma. "It may be that in the future, supermarkets may decide to kill all tags by default. That's a choice we leave to supermarkets."

Meanwhile, privacy just hasn't materialized as a concern at Metro.

"RFID is not something that shoppers notice, except for an enhanced shopping experience in terms of being able to find what they're looking for, with fewer empty shelves," says Albrecht von Truchsess. "And if shoppers didn't like it, we'd take it out." Case in Point: After a minor uproar over RFID tags embedded in Metro's loyalty cards, the company replaced the chips with standard magnetic strips, even though the chips reportedly only contained the same information printed on the card itself.

For its part, Wal-Mart insists that it was economics, not privacy concerns, that caused its reversal on smart shelves.

"We just can't understand the interest in one smart shelf that was never implemented," says Williams. "Smart shelves are simply impractical."[27]

For starters, says Williams, the notion of smart tags on individual products is simply cost-prohibitive.

At 20 cents and up, it's hard to justify a smart tag on a $3 Marie Callender frozen dinner, much less a 79-cent can of Green Giant green beans.

Scaled to a company the size of Wal-Mart, "that would be a very interesting, and very expensive experiment," says Forrester's Overby.[28]

And even if the tags reach 3 to 7 cents, the range generally perceived as the point where mass proliferation of smart tags is expected to accelerate, the company couldn't handle the data.

"We ship billions of products a day," says Williams. "The data would flood our systems; we wouldn't know what to do with it."

For now, at least, Wal-Mart's use of RFID will remain focused on turbocharging its world-renowned supply chain operations.

And that, industry watchers say, is enough to put every other retailer on notice. Today, retailers must wring every last efficiency out of the supply chain to remain competitive as Wal-Mart expands its operations around the world.

"A lot of competitors are being beat up on the supply chain side, and looking at their own RFID solutions," says Overby. "Wal-Mart's adoption of the technology is definitely the opening salvo."[29]

No fooling. Together with the likes of Prada, Stop & Shop, and especially, Extra, Wal-Mart and today's most innovative retailers are using wireless technologies to actively reshape what it means to shop in the twenty-first century. Which means if you can't make it to the store of tomorrow, don't worry.

It's already on its way to you.

Photo: John Abbott

Seth Godin:
Permission Marketing and
"My Own Private Idaho"

"Permission Marketing." "Purple Cows." "Idea Viruses."

As the progenitor of literally dozens of branding's most popular buzzwords, Seth Godin is virtually responsible for the entire lexicon of modern marketing.

A one-time Yahoo marketing VP, self-proclaimed "change agent," and author of bestsellers from *Permission Marketing* to *Unleashing the Idea Virus* to *All Marketers Are Liars: The Power of Telling Authentic Stories in a Low-Trust World*, Godin has long argued that successful companies must stifle the "antichange reflex" to build brands and create products that practically sell themselves.

Of course, harnessing change takes on new importance in an era when mobile technologies promise to extend the brand experience as never before.

RICK MATHIESON: Invoking Darwin, you've said the companies that are best able to adapt to change—to "make something happen"—will thrive. But you simultaneously argue that it's the small ideas and the low-cost, low-risk tests—evolutionary steps versus revolutionary steps—that often result in the largest ROI. What does that mean to companies that might be thinking about using mobile technologies to competitive advantage?

SETH GODIN: I don't think there is such a thing as revolution in nature. I think nature just does evolution, and it's revolution that gets all the good publicity. But it's pretty rare. Today, business is about irrevocable, irresistible, accelerating change that every company is wrestling with. It's about how innovation—mobile Internet technology or anything else—can change the ground rules of an entire industry.

What I'm telling companies is, don't sit around waiting until you have the perfect solution, because the perfect is the enemy of the good. In the enterprise space, I can easily imagine a sales force with fifty people, where you give ten people the sort of mobile toolkit that has the potential to increase their efficiency and gives them the freedom to test and to try things and to keep evolving. Pretty soon the other forty people will be yelling and clamoring and saying they want that stuff too. That's how change happens. And the companies that experiment like that will be able to identify what works, what doesn't, and what could lead to fundamental new ways to do business.

RM: What does this mean for consumer goods companies—the Pepsi-Colas of the world—who might be exploring ways to use the wireless Web to create remarkable experiences?

SG: The bad news about packaged goods companies is, they built their business model around something that was true a hundred years ago. Just because they were really successful and really profitable selling sugar water, doesn't mean that that's a guarantee it's going to be true in the future. Procter & Gamble is sucking wind, and will probably do so for the foreseeable future, because the mantra of supermarkets and television aren't what're driving our economy anymore, but that's what drives their companies. So when I look at, "Can I use my cell phone to buy something from a Coke machine?" I think that's sort of a cool innovation, and it's probably going to happen. But it's not going to change the dynamic of their business in a big way, in my humble opinion. If I were one of those packaged goods companies, I'd be scrambling as hard as I can to say, "How can we be in a completely different business five years from now?" If we're going to be in a completely different business five years from now, we better start now trying lots of little things so that we know what the big thing's going to be when we need it.

RM: What's an example of an innovation that could attract customers in the wireless age?

SG: Well, I can tell you what I'd like. I call it My Own Private Idaho. I want a device, maybe using Bluetooth, that I keep in my pocket. And I want it to tell every merchant, when I walk into their store, where I've been—sort of like [an Internet] cookie for the real world.

So now, if I'm in the mall and I just spent a fortune at Abercrombie and Fitch, and I walk in to the Gap, all those guys with the headsets instantly get word that I'm a big important customer, and they drop everything and run over and fawn over me like Julia Roberts in *Pretty Woman*. And then when I'm done browsing, I just throw the merchandise I want in the bag, and I leave—because the system knows who I am, and it knows how to charge me, the way Amazon remembers my one-click preferences, and I'm on to the next store.

I want to subscribe to that, and I will gladly permit the businesses my mobile carrier signs up with to know everything about me. I insist they know everything about me.

RM: As you know, these sorts of scenarios are becoming reality, sometimes connecting directly to consumers via mobile devices, sometimes transparently through RFID and other technologies. Why should companies be looking at wireless as a brand enabler?

SG: [As soon as businesses realize that wireless is] an asset that increases in value, as opposed to a wasting asset or a decreasing asset that you use up, then we end up with a whole different business dynamic.

In the future, the stuff that used to work isn't going to. That's nature. The early adopters in mobile are the ones who pay all the bills, because after you get to critical mass, it's all gravy. What do early adopters want? They want to save time, and they want to save money. If you can't figure out how to deliver that, wireless technologies aren't going to help. The secret is trying small pilots, new experiments, to see where things might go, so you can ride the next wave of innovation. Because as long as change is the only constant, evolving businesses will always win.

CHAPTER SIX

Service with a Stylus

Creating the Ultimate Guest Experience

Just ask Andrew Bradbury about the power of mBranding.

As wine director for chichi hot spot Aureole at Mandalay Bay Resort in Las Vegas, Bradbury has deployed new wireless technologies that are quickly redefining the way even the smallest service-based businesses run their operations and market themselves to customers.

At Aureole, guests peruse "eWine Books"—Wi-Fi–enabled tablet PCs that present a real-time list of the restaurant's 3,500 wines—complete with tasting notes, winery profiles, and other information.

In a particularly theatric flourish, servers, called "wine angels," are rigged up—Mission Impossible–style—to fly up and pluck everything from a $22 Stoneleigh Sauvignon Blanc to a $44,000 Château Petrus, from a sprawling, four-story wine tower or from one of six wine cellars.

The wireless link even integrates with the restaurant's POS and database systems, updating the otherwise unwieldy wine list when a given vintage sells out during the evening.

"Wireless is transforming the way we do business, and shaking up the entire industry," Bradbury says. "Wireless is helping me excite customers, build better relationships, and do things better than ever before."

And he's not alone.

For many marketers, shaping the brand experience means creating an environment conducive to selling more products. But for marketers in some industries, most notably travel and leisure, the experience *is* the product. And today, innovative businesspeople like Bradbury are increasingly using inexpensive mobile technologies to improve customer loyalty and to create the ultimate guest experience.

RESTAURANTS: THE (WIRELESS) HAND THAT FEEDS YOU

Servers at New York City's Republic restaurant, for instance, use handheld devices to send food and beverage orders wirelessly to the kitchen, reducing the number of jaunts through the restaurant's 4,000-square-foot-dining room.

As a result, the technology has cut the average table stay of the restaurant's 1,500 daily customers down to about 35 minutes, thanks to increased efficiency.

"We're on the less expensive end, so it's all about higher volume turnover," says manager Paul Downes. "The wireless ordering means more turnover, more people served—and more tips."

"Wireless eliminates foot traffic in and out of the kitchen or bar, so waiters can spend more time with diners," adds Lanny Nguyn of French-Asian restaurant L'anne, outside Chicago.[1]

At L'anne, waiters use PDAs to clock in and out, transmit orders, and process credit card transactions. "It saves on payroll because it cuts down on the total number of waiters you need," says Nguyn.

While industry analysts don't have a firm read on how much money is being spent by the restaurant industry on such wireless initiatives, they believe they're poised to take off.

Nearly 80 percent of restaurants have deployed PC–based POS

systems, according to solutions provider Ameranth Wireless.[2] With most such systems, it's a relatively straightforward proposition to integrate wireless devices.

"As restaurants move toward PCs with standard, off-the-shelf operating systems, a lot of these operating systems are embedded with hookups that make it pretty easy to deploy wireless," says Rob Grimes, chairman of Accuvia, a publishing, events, and consulting firm specializing in technology for the food service, retail, and hospitality industries. "Not a lot of restaurants are using these technologies now, but that's going to start changing."

L'anne's Nguyn, who maintains a day job as CFO of a wireless Web technology firm, designed her restaurant's wireless system for under $5,000 using custom software and five PDAs. Integration with the restaurant's POS system enables her to download reports so she knows whether the butternut squash is outselling the curried coconut with cilantro crème fraiche, or if it's time to order more Squab.

"It helps us with inventory control, and helps us customize the menu based on what sells best," she says.

Even $1,000 can go a long way toward creating a compelling customer experience. Both Starbucks and McDonald's report increased customer spend per visit by setting up simple Wi-Fi networks that allow customers with Web-enabled laptops to surf the Net or check e-mail. McDonald's already offers Wi-Fi at over 270 locations.[3] Starbucks, at over 3,100 locations.[4] A little more money will get you a digital jukebox, like those from Ecast and Pronto Networks, which doubles as a Wi-Fi hot spot.

"Used to be, you put a sign up advertising that you had air conditioning, and people came in. Now you put up a sign that says you have wireless Internet access instead," says Mick Mullen, owner of Scobies Sports Bar & Grill in Alameda, California, one of the pilot locations for an Ecast jukebox. "We not only saw our existing customers log on, we also saw new customers, who might not have otherwise come in, opening up their laptops and checking their e-mail while they enjoyed a drink."[5]

On the higher end, Aureole's Bradbury spent about $125,000 on hardware—including the wireless network, switches, charging stands, batteries, and Web tablets—and customized software, with about $30,000 to $40,000 on upgrades so far. But while the system has already contributed to $1 million in increased wine sales, Bradbury says he has bigger fish to fry.[6] See Figure 6-1.

Figure 6-1. Andrew Bradbury's eWinebook at chichi Aureole enables diners to peruse a real-time list of the restaurant's 3,500 wines—complete with tasting notes, winery profiles, and other information. Photo: Aureole Las Vegas.

"I'm only at about 50 percent of where I want to go with this technology," he says, adding that he's working to extend his service to Web-enabled cell phones so anyone who walks into the restaurant can use their own devices to place orders or review wines. Eventually, he says, it would be feasible to explore spinning off his wine list system into its own company, with a Web service that anyone can use, anywhere, on a subscription basis—even if they're at different restaurants.

HOTELS: WHERE WIRELESS IS INN VOGUE

From the tropical environs of the Fairmont Royal Pavilion in St. James to the Country Inn on the plains of Cheyenne, a burgeoning number of wireless initiatives promise to gain a competitive edge with the traveling public.

The epic Venetian Hotel in Las Vegas, for instance, has launched a wireless lodging management system that enables employees to conduct many operations of the 3,000-room hotel using wireless handheld devices.

Bellmen at the Venetian conduct wireless check-ins using handheld devices and miniature printers to swipe credit cards, activate room keys, and print out folios—without guests ever standing in line. Meanwhile, engineering, housekeeping, and other service employees are able to use PDA–like devices to wirelessly connect to the hotel's main POS and property management systems to handle just about any guest scenario—from taking a drink order for the $250-a-night newlyweds by the pool, to requesting more down pillows for the record company executive in a $1,000-a-night penthouse suite.

"There should never be a reason I can't serve a customer from anywhere on the property," adds the Venetian's CIO, Jack Braman. "The idea is to have something on my person that enables me to solve a guest issue or meet a guest need right there on the spot."[7]

Extending these and other wireless technologies within a self-service model, the Wall Street District Hotel has experimented with a system that enables its business-traveler clientele to check in by themselves, unlock room doors, and even request guest services using Bluetooth-enabled cell phones.

"Wireless check in is where travelers go 'Wow,'" says Tarun Malik, dean of academics at the Hospitality College at Johnson and Wales University in Charleston. "With all the security concerns at the airport, check-in bottlenecks, and all the hassles of travel, business people are fed up with standing in line."

With the solution the District has tested, road warriors first use their PCs to book a reservation by providing credit card and phone number information via a Web site. When they arrive, the system automatically recognizes their phones and sends a message confirming the reservation.

Once checked in, guests are able to unlock their room doors by entering a special code on their cell phones.

"It's a totally paperless transaction," says Frank Nicholas, managing director for the hotel. "Anything that helps cut down on time wasters is a huge differentiator for us."

While the hotel still has to iron out certain aspects of wireless check-in, "We believe wireless is the wave of the future," says Nicholas. And it's just the beginning. The hotel also offers citywide high-speed wireless Internet access through a partnership with MCI WorldCom. And guests can use their PDAs to download a Pocket Concierge that provides an interactive Zagat Restaurant Guide, a New York City subway map, a guide to local shopping from Saks to Bloomingdale's, and information on getting Broadway tickets to shows ranging from *Avenue Q* to *Wonderful Town*.

Some of the big hotel chains are even more aggressive. Inter-Continental Hotels, which operates 3,500 properties, including the Crowne Plaza, Holiday Inn, and the Staybridge Suites chains, has launched a wireless reservation system for frequent-guest Priority Club members who have WAP–enabled cell phones or PDAs.

After members provide a range of details, from credit cards to room preferences, via a PC, they can check availability, book reservations, extend stays, or make modifications to their room preferences—all from their PDA.

"Travelers no longer have to be in front of a PC, or call our reservation center," says Dell Ross, director of Internet business for InterContinental. "It's a benefit for our members, and we get the benefit of extra odds that we'll get their next stay."

In 2004, the company opened a prototype for a new generation of Holiday Inn hotels that applies innovative new wireless point-of-sale technologies. Guests at the Holiday Inn Gwinnett Center in Duluth, Georgia, just north of Atlanta, can use an "e-menu" tablet PC at tables in the hotel restaurant. The tablet provides customers with an electronic menu of food and beverage offerings in the establishment, and contains pictures of each dish, along with ingredients. Customers can view nutritional information about each item, and recommendations for meals that meet the needs of diets ranging from Weight Watchers to South Beach. While sitting at a table, guests can check e-mail, read news, and play games. And corporate travelers can connect to airline carriers to purchase airline tickets or to arrange for a cab ride. Guests can even use the tablet to pay for their food, with transactions displayed in multiple currencies.

Best of all, guests can respond to surveys or register complaints on the spot, enabling hotel management to fix issues immediately, rather than finding out about the problem long after a guest has checked out, as is the case with most paper-based surveys.

"With this hotel we believe Holiday Inn has arrived at the perfect convergence of technology and brand authenticity that will define the hotel experience of the future," Mark Snyder, senior vice president of brand management for Holiday Inn Hotels & Resorts, declared at the hotel's grand opening.[8]

Hilton Hotels has announced plans to launch a similar system for its Hilton HHonors members. And Fairmont Hotels Worldwide has spent upward of $2 million to link forty-two properties together in one giant, unified network infrastructure with integrated provisioning and allocation capabilities that could soon include all-new forms of wireless services.

Today, each of the chain's city center and resort locations features a minimum of one to a dozen Wi-Fi hot spots that enable guests to surf the Web by the pool or in the lobby. And wireless Internet access is available just about everywhere—including guest rooms—at Fairmont's venerable Plaza Hotel in New York City. According to Fairmont senior vice president Tim Aubrey, the company's unified infrastructure could one day give guests the ability to order room service, view videos, listen to music, review their own folio, and check out of the hotel, all from a PDA–like device.

"Since the infrastructure is run to all our properties, we have the ability to propagate capabilities throughout all our chains instantaneously," he says. "If we can get all 20,000 guests online, and tie them into services rendered from the relevant employee base, you have some powerful guest services opportunities."

Still, for all the bells and whistles these new-fangled technologies bring to serving guests, their real potential may lie in behind-the-scenes hotel management. Carlson Hospitalities Worldwide, which operates the Regent, Radisson, and Country Inn & Suites chains, among others, recently launched a wireless system that connects 150 corporate employees, hotel executives, and management companies in 140 countries to Carlson's $20 million MIS and reservation system.

Dubbed Mobile Access to Carlson Hospitality, Version Two (MACH-2), this system enables executives and franchisees to choose from over fifty real-time business metrics—customer complaints, check-in rates, average revenue per room, sales, housekeeping performance—that are viewable via HP iPaq Pocket PCs and, soon, cellular phones.

"Rather than looking in the rearview mirror of a weekly or monthly report, you're alerted to changing business dynamics in real time if a certain metric is off track today, or this hour," says Carlson CIO Scott Heintzeman. "Suddenly, you've moved to a highly proactive way of managing your property."[9]

Of course, these types of wireless capabilities have been a growing trend among hoteliers for some time.

Today 10 to 15 percent of hotels offer guests some kind of wireless Internet access, usually through proprietary WLAN or public hot spots in lobbies, bars, conference rooms, and even by the pool.

According to research from IDC, the number of hot spots in public spaces has grown from just 50,000 in 2003 to well over 85,000 today—accounting for over $1 billion in spending—mostly through deployments in hotels, convention centers, airports, and cafes.[10]

That growth, experts say, is fueled by the declining costs associated with setting up necessary access points, or gateways, that can be used for guest Internet access, point of sale, or operations management applications.

"When you factor in the cost of adding wireless on top of existing management infrastructure, it's really minimal," says Fairmont's Aubrey, who says his company spent about $1,000 each on one to six such access points in each of his hotels, plus about $200 per guest room where wireless access is available. "The cost of deployment is quite low compared to the benefit of doing so."

"You have to keep up with the Joneses," says Malik. "In the near future, hotels from the high end to the low end are going to suffer in comparison to those that are using these wireless technologies to better react to guest needs."

THEME PARKS: MICKEY GOES MOBILE

Facing fierce competition for family entertainment dollars, theme parks and other entertainment and learning centers are exploring the use of mobile technologies to improve service, increase revenues-per-visit, and personalize the park experience.

Not surprisingly, the Disney Corporation figures prominently into the equation. According to *CIO Insight*, the Mouse House is using Disneyworld in Orlando as a test location for several new wireless innovations.[11]

Among the most compelling: A 10.5-inch stuffed doll—called Pal Mickey—that acts as a wireless-enabled virtual tour guide, providing trivia about the park, tips on which rides have the shortest lines, and information on the latest parades and events.

An infrared sensor in the doll's nose interacts with any of 500 beacons placed inconspicuously around the park, enabling park attendants to transmit the latest ride and event information to visitors in near real time. A cache of over one hundred minutes of prerecorded factoids is triggered depending on location or time of day. "Say, 'Fantasmic!' will be starting in about an hour," the doll might shout, reminding guests about the park's nightly laser-fireworks-waterworks extravaganza.[12] Or the doll might giggle, "Pirates are sneaking around," just in time to turn a corner where characters from Pirates of the Caribbean are signing autographs. And while kids wait in line, they can play interactive games.

Disney is also using text messaging to customize visitors' stays. Visitors who have provided information about vacation preferences can have alerts sent to their cell phones about attractions they might like, or reminders about dining reservations, scheduled events, or more.

"Enough people are bringing their cell phones in that we have new ways to take the hassle out of their park experience," Disney

CIO Roger Berry told the magazine. "For example, if you have certain characters you're interested in, and you want to know when they're coming out in the park, we can let you know that."[13]

Not to be outdone, museums like the Port Discovery Museum in Baltimore are also making use of wireless digital docents to make the museum-going experience more interactive, more educational—and more fun.

At Port Discovery, one recent exhibit enabled kids to use a special BlackBerry pager that would then lead them through a series of interactive activities integrated with twelve exhibits about ancient Egypt.

Linked to a wireless network backed by an extensive content management system, the pager—dubbed a Kid's Club Communicator—cast kids in the role of 1920s-era archeologists on a mission to find the tomb of a fictional pharaoh.

In one exhibit area, the pager displayed hieroglyphics for kids to decipher by consulting a wheel containing the hieroglyphics and their corresponding English letters.

In another, kids were asked to identify the deity pictured on the Communicator display that does not match the deities represented on a wall. If the correct image was selected, the device sent a signal to the network, which then displayed booming sound effects and an animated video about the next step of the adventure, shown on a wall-mounted plasma screen.

Kids earned points for each mission completed. And once they had earned one hundred points, they could send instant messages to friends in other areas of the exhibition.

"It's absolutely magical," says Amy O'Brien, a tech expert who led the project for the museum. "It gives kids control of their personal experience based on who they are, where they are in the exhibition, and what they're most interested in learning."[14]

Sometimes, the brand experience enabled by the technology simply helps parents keep track of their kids. At Legoland Denmark, one of Europe's largest amusement parks, RFID wristbands have helped locate approximately 1,600 kids who have become separated from their parents.[15] Hundreds of readers around the park ping the wristbands as kids walk by. At 2.5 million square feet, the location network that enables this system is the largest in the world.

PLANES, TRAINS, AND AUTOMOBILES: HASSLE-FREE TRAVEL TAKES OFF

For travel and leisure companies, the journey is often as important as the destination.

By now, most major transportation companies have deployed Wi-Fi network hot spots for Internet-hungry travelers. American Airlines, for instance, has deployed hot spots in all of its frequent-flier lounges nationwide, and Boeing's in-flight Connexion service offers satellite-based high-speed Internet access to 1,500 commercial aircraft.

Passengers can check e-mail, surf the Internet, and access corporate intranets. Since the access is facilitated through a service portal, passengers can directly access travel schedules and mileage plans, as well as arrange for ground transportation and hotel accommodations. Though the service is fairly new, Connexion is projecting sales of over $3 billion over the next ten years as demand for in-flight connectivity builds.[16]

"[These] are all things that passengers want and need to do while mobile," says spokesperson Terrance Scott. "Airlines benefit as well because they can offer tailored, personalized customer service to passengers, which translates to brand differentiation and potential share shift in the market by luring new or repeat passengers."

Meanwhile, Amtrak offers wireless Internet access on train routes through the Northeast Corridor and Chicago metro areas, as well as in Northern California. And many a New York City cab offers wireless access from seat-back consoles. These services are all part of an effort by Internet darling Yahoo to expand consumer adoption of wireless technologies and leverage its brand into the mobile medium. Passengers can surf the Web and access many of Yahoo's most popular services, including Yahoo mail, news, weather, and sports.

"Our strategy is to put these devices in an experience that is fairly common—commuting, or riding on plane, or at a fun event— and let them experience using this access to surf the Web wire- lessly," says Christopher Wu, head of product strategy for Yahoo Mobile.[17]

But most experts agree that it's the airline industry that stands to benefit most from wireless tech. Especially useful for harried business travelers, simple airport- or in-flight-based Wi-Fi access en- ables easy e-mail access or Internet surfing while sprinting between gates or munching peanuts and sipping colas at 20,000 feet.

An increasingly number of voice-based cell phone calls is on the way, too. Airbus plans to install an in-flight phone network on its aircraft by 2006, enabling passengers to place calls from their own cell phones, instead of the older, more expensive brick-sized phones embedded in seat-backs.[18] But that's not all good news. The ambi- ent noise of airplane cabins requires cell phone users to speak very loudly to have conversations. Which means flights may seem longer, and more grating than ever, when passengers crammed into tiny seats are captive to conversations held by people shouting into handsets.

Indeed, perhaps the real value of wireless lies not in serving passengers en route, but in helping them better manage their flight itineraries on the ground.

United Airlines, for instance, offers a wireless service that en- ables customers to receive the latest information on departure times, gate changes, or cancellations direct from their PDA or cell phone. The service even rebooks reservations if weather forces the airline to cancel a flight. And wireless arrival notifications can be sent via cell phones to people picking up airline passengers at the gate.

For its part, low-fare airline JetBlue has taken the first step to the "hurdle free" airport with its implementation of a wireless curb- side check-in system during peak travel periods. The system, the first of its kind in the United States, allows designated JetBlue staff to check-in passengers, print boarding passes, and check luggage virtually anywhere inside or outside the terminal.

"Waiting in line only adds to the stress of flying during peak travel times," says Jeff Cohen, former JetBlue vice president and CIO.[19] "This unique system not only cuts frustration and saves time for our passengers, it helps keep operations running smoothly and on time, by allowing us to get passengers, especially late ones, checked-in and to the plane without delay."

Wireless tech is even helping mitigate that age-old scourge of air travel: Delta Airlines is developing wireless technology for tracking lost luggage, which could potentially save the airline over $100 million a year in costs—and who knows how much in passenger irritation—by 2007.[20]

Of course, if Delta's baggage handlers wanted to boost those savings even higher, they could always call Aureole's Bradbury. When his "wine angels" get tired of serving Bordeaux, maybe they could go fetch our baggage.

Photo: Kathy Tarantola

Tom Peters:
The Gospel According to St. Peters

Part polemicist, part unabashed cheerleader, Tom Peters says the future of business will be driven by those who laugh in the face of today's play-it-safe corporate mind-set and fearlessly allow themselves to "screw up, think weird, and throw out the old business playbooks."

Of course, he's always had a sensationalist streak. With the success of his best-selling books, *In Search of Excellence,* *The Brand You,* and half-dozen others, Peters invented the manager-as-rock-star ethos of the 1980s, and the "Me, Inc." entrepreneurialism of the 1990s. The *Los Angeles Times* has called him "the father of the postmodern corporation." And today, companies pay the sixty-year-old rabble-rouser up to $50,000 for a one-hour speech in hopes of gleaning some secret to success in twenty-first-century business. In Peters's eyes, tomorrow's increasingly messy and chaotic world belongs to those who embrace "creative destruction"; nimble, creative innovators who go beyond the production of mere products and services to master the all-powerful customer experience.

RICK MATHIESON: One of your major themes is the power of disruptive technology. How do you think the emergence of mobile technologies and pervasive computing can best be put to use to enhance the way organizations operate?

TOM PETERS: The most important thing I can say is, 'I don't know.' And anybody who says they do know is an idiot, and you may quote me on that. And what I mean by this is, I think the change is so profound, particularly relative to the extremely young men and extremely young women who will be peopling organizations ten years from now, that I think we've got to make the whole damn thing up anew. I refuse to consider that I'm the genius who has mapped the path out.

I think I've said some things that are not silly. But as Peter Drucker said, we're still looking for the Copernicus of the New Organization. I quote a lot of people, like David Weinberger, who I adore, who wrote this book called *Small Pieces Loosely Joined*, and Howard Rheingold with *Smart Mobs*, and so on. I think that there are a whole lot of very smart people who are painting some very interesting pictures right now. But to say that somebody has painted the correct picture is a gross exaggeration, and it sure as hell isn't me.

RM: Some of your most exciting themes have always been around branding and creating memorable customer experiences. Today, when companies look at new technology, how should we move the discussion about technology from creating efficiency to creating experiences—the value that technology can bring to your brand?

TP: Obviously, even though it's technologically driven, Apple/Pixar has always created great experiences, albeit at a price.

Look, we're moving to a more and more ethereal society where the manufactured product is less significant than before. And as we continue to shift these very expensive jobs offshore, the question, the issue, the struggle is,

"What's left?" And presumably what's left increasingly is the very high value–added stuff, and that value-added stuff is the stuff Steve Jobs has understood since the beginning of time.

RM: In your recent book, *Re-Imagine: Business Excellence in a Disruptive Age*, you write about your own tombstone and wanting to be remembered as "a player." What does that mean in the disruptive age when wireless is redefining just about everything?

TP: I'm older than you are; that's the easy answer. People at sixty think about things that people who are significantly less therein don't. I'm almost in a sappy way taking advantage of my age here. But I think the big message is: This whole new technology thing—whether we're talking Napster, whether we're talking the Recording Industry of America, whether we're talking wireless, whether we're talking about war with terrorists—[means] we're engaged in this exceptionally energetic process of redefinition, which will generate some number of winners, and lots of losers. And participation vigorously therein is what it's all about.

I look at all the people who are sour, including Silicon Valley people who thought God put them on Earth to make $1 million by the age of twenty-six, if not $10 million, and I say, how cool to be part of this. I love some of those who have made a trillion dollars and some who are less well-known who have lost a trillion dollars, but were vigorously engaged in the fray. [It's all] about those in the fray at a time of truly dramatic change. Something quite exceptional is going down. In the best sense of the word—and not said with naïveté or rose-colored glasses—it's a very cool time to be alive.

CHAPTER SEVEN

No Wires, New Rules

The Wireless World's New Social Fabric—
and What It Means to Marketers

Q: What do party-going teenagers have in common with Al-Qaeda terrorists?

A: They're among a growing list of groups—including environmental activists, political demonstrators, even celebrity stalkers—who are using new mobile technologies to organize collective action on a scale never before possible.

Futurist Howard Rheingold, author of *Smart Mobs: The Next Social Revolution*, was among the earliest to uncover this monumental sociological shift. By applying principles of computer science, economics, and anthropology, Rheingold uncovered what he calls "Generation Txt"—young, mobile netizens who use cell phones, pagers, and PDAs to coordinate protests, stage raves, and even overthrow governments. All just by sending text messages.

In 1999, the protesters at a World Trade Organization gathering used dynamically updated Web sites and cell phones to coordinate demonstrations during the "Battle of Seattle."

In 2004, Spanish citizens enraged over the war in Iraq used e-mail and text messages to coordinate efforts to oust the government of President Jose Maria Aznar in national elections.

It's even been reported that the 9-11 hijackers used pagers to coordinate their sinister efforts.

But beyond such world-changing efforts lays a much more common—and infinitely more entertaining—pursuit: young people connecting with other young people to commiserate, have fun, and even make a little mayhem.

Barhoppers coordinate with friends and even exchange photos of the evening's events—and possible dates—using camera phones. Angst-ridden fourteen-year-olds use e-mail and SMS to post Web logs, or "blogs"—online public diaries—about their lives, loves, and acne-inspired horror stories for millions (or maybe just their clique) to read. And classroom-bound students use text messaging to send each other answers during tests.

Today, over 50 percent of all teenagers under the age of seventeen have cell phones, and most "are able to text in their pocket without seeing their phone," says Derick Forde, CEO of Cellbusters, a company that detects and prevents outbound cell phone calls for security, privacy, and other reasons. "They are able to do it almost blindfolded."[1]

And they seem to be doing it everywhere, all the time. Worldwide, person-to-person messaging via SMS, MMS, and IM already accounts for well over $30 billion a year in revenues for cell phone carriers—a figure that could top $92 billion by 2007.[2, 3]

In a visual twist on ringtones, messaging exhibitionists will soon even be sharing their missives for all within eyesight. Some new cell phones project visible text messages when the user waves a handset in the air; messages appear to float just above the user, for all within thirty feet to see—perfect for communicating with friends across crowded rooms.[4]

Call it Swarming, Posse Pinging, or sometimes just Dialing for Dates. By whatever name, these new forms of social connectivity are transforming the way an entire generation of mobile consumers interacts with each other and their world.

"You have to really look at the simplicity of the applications for the PC in 1980, or the Internet in 1990, to understand that the simple, early clues point in a direction—and that direction is toward a world where people are able to act collectively as never before," says Rheingold. "Because when you combine the social communications aspect with the ability to exchange content with each other, that becomes another medium, in the way that adding the World Wide Web to the Internet made it a new medium for many people. That's what's happening in the mobile arena today."[5]

Throughout this book, we've explored some of the ways the world's most powerful brands are using the mobile medium to connect with consumers in exciting new ways. But the more profound shift is how these mobile consumers are communicating with one another. And as you're about to see, this virtual public space is rich with possibilities for the very savviest of marketers, and fraught with danger for everyone else.

Here's a look at some early fashions, fads, and frenzies—and what they mean to you.

SOCIAL NETWORKING: MOVING TO THE GROOVE

When twenty-eight-year-old Manhattanite Dennis Crowley wants to party, he can always count on 10,000 of his closest friends.

Like many young tech industry professionals caught up in the dot-com implosion of 2000, Crowley's sizable circle of friends, colleagues, and acquaintances found themselves laid off and drifting apart—their social networks crumbling as the number of familiar faces at favorite nightclubs and watering holes grew fewer.

So Crowley did something about it. Drawing on his programming skills, he developed a rudimentary wireless system that would allow the first of his buddies to venture out on, say, Wednesday night, to broadcast his location to the whole gang so they could all meet up.

"For the first couple of years, there were maybe twenty-five of us using it, and then we started to look back at what had happened in the last couple of years—text messaging having become ubiquitous, and everyone was starting to use camera phones, which I knew because I was even getting camera phone messages from my mom," he says.

Venturing back to school for a master's degree in Interactive Telecommunications from New York University, Crowley teamed up with classmate Alex Rainert, 28, to turn his idea—called Dodgeball.com—into a formal service as part of their thesis project.

"We looked at the online social networking space—Friendster, Meet-up, Nerve.com—and we asked, how could we take some of the lessons learned from that and apply it to [the mobile space]?" he says, referring to online social networking sites that enable friends, and friends of friends, to synch up and plan get-togethers via the wireline Internet. By contrast, Dodgeball would be designed specifically to help you get it on when you're on the go.

By the time of its formal launch in April of 2004, over 5,500 New Yorkers, along with 3,000 users in San Francisco, Chicago, and Los Angeles, and a few thousand others scattered across twenty other cities, had signed up for the free service. Since then, Dodgeball has evolved into a social networking cause célèbre for hip young singles on the move.

Here's how it works. You pull up a seat at Tom & Jerry's on Elizabeth and Houston at 7:30 P.M. You send a message: "@Tomn jerry to nyc@dodgeball.com." Instantly, your entire buddy list receives a text message about your whereabouts. But Dodgeball doesn't stop there. In addition to pinging your friends, the system also pings all the friends of your friends that are within ten blocks. They receive a message such as, "Joe is over at Tom n Jerry's. You know Joe through Karen. Why don't you stop over and say hi." These friends of friends often send pictures via camera phone to each other so they can find each other in crowded bars.

"It's like a shortcut," Alexander Clemens, a thirty-something political consultant in San Francisco, told the *New York Times*. "All it takes is one quick note to tell friends where the party's at."[6]

Which is all very cool. But there's more. Since users sign up for service through the Dodgeball Web site, where they've included profiles and, if they wish, photos, they can browse other members and build "crush lists"—up to five crushes at a time. Whenever one of those crushes comes within ten blocks, the system gives you a heads up. The crush gets a message: "Hey, this guy Joe is over at Tom & Jerry's. He thinks you're cute. Why don't you stop by and say hi?" Joe gets a more enticing, if more cryptic, alert: "One of your crushes is within ten blocks. We won't tell you where, we just told them where you are, so make yourself presentable."

Which is to say, this particular wireless wingman is less about creating "smart mobs" and more about making booty calls.

"The moment we turned this feature on, it was like 1:30 Tuesday morning, and ten minutes later, the first message got sent out to a friend of mine," says Crowley. "He goes down the street to meet the girl, who's just realized she received a photo on her phone, and was showing it to her friend. There was this strange, awkward moment like, 'Hey, you're the guy in the photo, this is kind of weird.' But they had a drink together. That was the first time it ever happened, and now it happens all the time."

What It Means to Marketers

Advertisers have always been the bête noires of social networking.

But for certain lifestyle brands, Dodgeball's unique blend of cell phones and singles seems like a natural fit, as long as they tread carefully.

"We're the number one users of the system in terms of number of friends, and the last thing I want to build is something that's going to cause me not to want to use it," says Crowley.

Enter: Absolut vodka, the first major brand to take notice of Dodgeball, testing the nascent service as a way to reach affluent young hipsters when they're most likely to be enticed to indulge in the marketer's product.

In addition to sponsoring SMS messages to remind subscribers to use Dodgeball when they're out, Absolut tested a campaign called "Flavor the Summer," in which Dodgeball members could click on a banner on the Dodgeball home page to add the beverage as a "friend" to their network. Once members opted in, Absolut would send messages to users asking them to tell Dodgeball about their current whereabouts in exchange for information about nearby events, happenings, happy hour venues, after-hours venues and more. See Figure 7-1.

For example, every Tuesday at 6 P.M., the system would cross-reference a weather database and send users a message that reads, say:

> What a gorgeous day! Reply with @venuename telling us where u are. Dodgeball and Absolut will send the closest outdoor patio

When they reply, members would then receive a follow-up message based on their location:

> Dodgeball & Absolut suggest you work on your tan and enjoy a cocktail at The Water Club (at 30ᵗʰ Street)

Figure 7-1. Absolut is one of the first major brands to test out social networking services like Dodgeball as a way to reach hip young consumers on the go. Photo: Dr. Jaeger.com.

"Our consumers are more and more mobile, and we need to look at alternate message delivery vehicles to reach them," says Lorne Fisher, spokesperson for Absolut. "If Absolut is top-of-mind, it may be a way to generate more 'call' in bars, restaurants, liquor stores, and so on."

In the future, look for social networking capabilities to be built into a number of products. Newfangled electronic T-shirts, available from high-tech retailer Cyberdog, for instance, come with a postcard-sized passive-matrix display that enables the wearer to flash messages of up to thirty-two characters across his or her chest. Combine that with an RFID tag within a wirelessly connected environment, or even just built-in Bluetooth, and whenever a member of a particular social network comes within range, the shirts could flash messages to facilitate a hookup. All sponsored by a mutually preferred brand name, of course.

MOBILITY + BLOGGING = MOBLOGGING

Alternatively hailed as the "End of Big Media As We Know It," or dismissed as the solipsistic ramblings of (typically) left-leaning political news junkies, blogging has hit the mainstream consciousness in recent years. While the early days of the Internet were about posting your own Web page, it's increasingly about running your own blog—online homesteads from which bloggers post their thoughts, jokes, breaking news, and links to sites they think are interesting. Readers can post comments, and ongoing conversations ensue throughout the entire community of interest.

According to research from the Pew Internet and American Life Project, only about 7 percent of adult Internet users have created Web blogs. Only about 27 percent of online Americans have ever checked out a single blog. And nearly 62 percent of U.S. Internet users have no idea what a blogs is.[7] But that's not the point. These digital soapboxes democratize media so everyone who wants one can have a voice in what has become popularly known as the "blogosphere."

"When you look around at today's generation, it's all about me. Look at me; my life is special. I count; I matter," says Chris Hoar, founder of blogging site Textamerica.com. "Even though they're not a celebrity or a big figure in politics or whatever, having a blog means you still count, you matter."

According to the Pew research, the average blogger is roughly twenty-five years old, and is more likely than others to use instant messaging, play games, and download music. For many, the attraction of blogging is an unedited, unfiltered, virtual pulpit from which to hold forth on whatever topics interest them—from geopolitics to sustainable agriculture to chess. There's even an entire genre called "meta blogging," devoted to covering the world of blogs and the blogging bloggers who blog them.

"Beyond the pure fun of creating something to share with others locally or globally, the Internet is living up to its promise to empower the individual," says Pew researcher Amanda Lenhart. "The world is changing when anyone with a modem can do the same thing as the most sprawling media company, the most powerful politician, or highest-paid entertainer."[8]

As a result, "citizen journalists" frequently scoop major news outlets, or doggedly pursue stories until mainstream news outlets are forced to take notice. Russ Kick's memoryhole.org was among several that published banned photographs of flag-draped caskets of United States soldiers killed in Iraq as they arrived at Dover Air Force Base, for example. And in the wake of the 2004 presidential elections, political parties have embraced blogs as a powerful way to evangelize their cause and raise gobs of money.

Some blogs are even emerging as commercial successes: Mini-media mogul Nick Denton runs a gaggle of subversively quirky gossip blogs, including, among others, Wonkette, a snarky look at modern politics; Gawker, for those obsessed with the world of pop culture; Jalopnik, a site about suped-up cars, and many others. These sites have earned quite a following. Wonkette, for instance, garners an estimated 430,000 page views per month.[9] And though Denton is mum on the matter, it's estimated that each of his blogs fetches $5,000 to $10,000 per month each in advertising.[10]

Without a doubt, mainstream media has become obsessed with

the handful of well-read properties that, on occasion, outshine some of the brightest lights in journalism. But the vast majority of blogs are designed for the most micro of niche markets—family, friends, coworkers—and far more personal in their ambitions. Typical blogs feature images from Christmas, showing off a new car, reveling in a hobby, or debating the artistic merits of a favorite movie or television show.

Like the computers they seem glued to, bloggers are increasingly playing a part in the mobile revolution. So-called mobile blogging—or "moblogging"—is finding practitioners updating a traditional text-based blog via SMS, or creating a photo, video, or audio blog via their cell phones.

Take thirty-four-year-old Web programmer Mike Popovic of Westbrook, Maine. In October 2002, after trying the earliest "hiptop" all-in-one personal organizer-e-mail-Internet device, formally known as the T-Mobile Sidekick, Popovic became addicted when he was able to use a camera attachment to take photo images of those had-to-be-there moments, and then post them instantly on his blog.

"I was like, 'Wow, I can post pictures from where I am right now,' while I'm on a hike, or whatever—it was a lot of fun," he says.

His images caught the attention of other hiptop enthusiasts, and within months, a growing community of nearly 1,000 "hiploggers" were posting their images on a site that came to be known as Hiptop Nation.

"We have a lot of people trying experimental photography, close-ups of certain things, different angles, signs, and things they probably wouldn't have taken a picture of with a real camera," he says.

Indeed, Hiptop Nation's eclectic mix of postage-sized images (and associated commentary) capture life's stolen moments, glimpses of forgotten time seen through loose-knit streams of consciousness and captured in stills that, in some cases, would never otherwise be committed to film or disk space.

"The more you do this, the more you develop an eye for it, and a sense for it. When I go to an event, or when I'm just walking down the street, I notice things, pick out interesting little details on things that normally I would not have even registered consciously. And I think, 'That would be a cool shot,' or 'That's a little bit interesting, you should put that up on the blog.'"

Indeed, it's here that differences emerge between mobloggers and their wireline brethren. While traditional bloggers tend to expound on the evils or virtues of some given subject, moblogging correlates experience with points of interest in the real world, annotating everything from bars and restaurants to beaches to the outback and even entire cities. Not to mention people's lives.

"I don't think soccer moms and NASCAR dads have thirty minutes to write an online journal," says Textamerica's Chris Hoar. "But people always take pictures, and they always want to share them. They'll show themselves happy, sober, drunk, or doing whatever—no holds barred. This is a very easy way for them to do that." To that end, Textamerica has attracted 500,000 users, 110,000 who spend $5.99 to $9.99 per month to post moblogs, and about 400,000 who just view and comment. Similar sites, like moblog.com, yafro .com, buzznet.com, and moblogUK.net are popping up every day.

Meanwhile, audio blogs enable bloggers to offer voice commentary on their favorite subjects, and newer phenomena, like "podcasting," are opening up whole new possibilities.

A podcast is a kind of audio recording that can be posted on a Web site so listeners can download it to an Apple iPod or an MP3 player and take it on the go. The technology for podcasts was developed in August 2004 by, of all people, 1980s-era MTV video jockey Adam Curry and programmer friend David Winer. It's become a veritable craze, spawning over 4,000 grassroots podcasts worldwide, including the likes of "Why Fish," a paean to North Dakota walleye fishing; "Grape Radio," a *Sideways*-like buddy show about wine drinking; and numerous "Godcasts," or podcasts with religious content.

Factor in the video blogging, or "vlogging," and suddenly, we're talking about a world where everyone can have their own narrowcast television or radio show, produced at a live event and available to anyone, anytime.

"We are insanely social creatures," adds David Weinberger, author of *Small Pieces, Loosely Joined: A Unified Theory of the Web.* "We want to connect with other people. We've always been able to do that, but we've been limited by, in many ways, geography in our ability to do so. Now we're not limited. We have an infinitely expandable, unmanaged public space. And we are flooding it with as many different ways of connecting as we can."[11]

What It Means to Marketers

Whether they realize it or not, the democratization of digital media represented by blogging, chat rooms, and other ongoing, online conversations are of utmost importance to marketers. That's because, chances are, there are online communities devoted to debating the merits of you, your company, and your products—for better or worse.

"It used to be that we assumed that [companies] were the only source of information about their products, and now we assume that they're the worst source of information for their products. We have alternatives," says Weinberger. Whether marketers know it or not, "their marketing brochure is actually Google, and so whatever comes up in Google is what customers read."

But therein likes tremendous opportunity. Blogs, chat rooms, and other online venues may represent an incredibly affordable way to communicate with hard-core fans and customers.

When Microsoft was preparing to launch a new version of MSN Search, for instance, select bloggers were among those invited to an event at the company's Redmond headquarters to kick the tires and spread the word to technorati everywhere.[12] CEOs Richard Edelman of PR giant Edelman has his own blog, as do prominent executives at Yahoo, Monster.com, and Maytag.[13] Even Hollywood studios are blogging: Fox Searchlight used a blog by TV star Zach Braff to create buzz for the writer-director-actor's independent film, *Garden State.*[14]

Not surprisingly in these early days of adoption, the high-tech industry is having particular success with blogs.

"I don't have the advertising budget to get our message to, for instance, Java developers working on handset applications for the medical industry," says Sun Microsystems CEO Jonathan Schwartz, whose geeky blog attracts 35,000 avid readers per month.[15] "But one of our developers, just by taking time to write a blog, can do a great job getting our message out to a fanatic readership."

Now imagine the power that mobile devices bring to this endeavor. Field sales and service teams could access blogs, or newer online venues like "wikis," for information. Based on the Hawaiian word "wiki wiki" for "quick," wikis are a kind of online whiteboard or notebook where users can collaborate and share knowledge.

Now, field teams can always get the latest product information, or even post an image of, say, a broken machine axle, and ask other team members for information on how to fix it so the customer is up and running again fast.

Public relations and crisis management communicators could use moblogs to post images of say, a drug company CEO in the midst of implementing a massive recall, or a car manufacturer conducting a road test for a hot new concept car. General Motors, for instance, has long used its "Fastlane Blog" to communicate with customers. And it even started podcasting live events, beginning with the launch of the Cadillac DTS and Buick Lucerne luxury sedans at the Chicago Auto Show.

Viral marketers could use fans to propagate short clips or vlogs of short films such as Honda's "Cog" or BMW Films' "The Hire" series to friends' handsets, where they could spread like wildfire.

"Some of the most successful and memorable Web-based campaigns have been the ones that individual end users have passed along from one to the other. And I think we're going to see more and more of that in the mobile world," says Joe Laszlo, a senior analyst for Jupiter Research.

"When we get to the stage where people feel more comfortable sending pictures to other people's mobiles, as opposed to e-mail addresses or uploading them to Web servers, I think that's going to be a signal that we're much closer to a world where people will also be receptive to, and interested in, passing on other kinds of content. I think that's the key thing for making a viral campaign work in the mobile world."

And don't forget those sponsorships, which enable companies to foster brand affinity while learning firsthand what drives their customer base. Nick Denton's assorted blogs, remember, are all advertising-supported. In fact, auto-oriented Jalopnik is exclusively sponsored by Audi, marking one of the first such arrangements of its kind.[16]

"It's about really connecting at the grassroots level with customers," says Chris Hoar. "Instead of posting ad banners on a site that say, 'Here's my product, buy it,' it's more about, 'Hey, we're going to help pay for this site. We're going to help make it really cool. And we're going to give prizes for people who submit the best pictures.'"

Or, as Lydia Snape, Internet services director for New York ad agency Renegade Marketing, put it to *Business 2.0*: "Done right, consumers will do all the marketing for the company—forwarding the information they found to their friends and encouraging others to visit."[17]

HIGH-TECH HIJINKS

An early example of extending the virtual world into the real world in the interest of fun and games, the phenomena known as "flash mobs" gained worldwide attention as mobility's first social craze.

At their most essential, flash mobs are collective acts of weirdness that find hundreds of people coordinating using e-mail, cell phones, IM, and SMS to congregate on some public space to engage in some bizarre behavior—say, a two-minute game of duck-duck-goose in a Chicago-area park, or standing on one leg and coughing in front of a delicatessen in downtown Manhattan—before disappearing just as quickly as they appeared.

But there are indications the flash mob phenomenon has peaked, replaced by other opportunities for fun.

Case in point: Today, the rising popularity of camera phones, PDAs, and GPS devices is putting a high-tech twist on the age-old game of treasure hunt.

One variation, called "geocaching," involves "treasure chests" hidden in parks, cities, or the wilderness. Treasure hunters use portable GPS devices to lock into the coordinates of these "caches," or boxes of goodies. Often, the boxes contain treasures like CDs, books, maps, games, jewelry, even money. Some contain digital cameras to snap photos of the find, or a logbook. When the treasure hunters find the cache, they leave it in its place for others to find.

Two basic rules apply: If you find a cache, you must leave a log entry. Another: If you take something out of the cache, you have to put something new in.

First played in 2000, a nationwide community has arisen from the adventure game, centered on the geocaching.com Web site, where players can enter a zip code to find the longitude and latitude of cached treasures in their area. It's estimated that regional groups of players have already hidden 13,000 caches across all 50 states and 200 countries.

According to geocaching.com, the locations of caches typically reflect the daring of the individual group's founder: A cache hidden on the side of a rocky cliff may require climbing equipment to reach it, while one hidden underwater may require scuba gear. Once caches are in place, groups host geocaching events, and even charter adventure vacations centered on the game.

As avid geocacher T.J. Couch, 33, of Lake Magdalene, Florida, put it to the *Saint Petersburg Times*: "I enjoy the outdoors, but I'd never be sitting on the couch on a Saturday saying, 'Let's go to Starkey Nature Path, and walk the trails,'" he says. "But knowing there's an adventure outside there, I'd walk through waist-deep swamp water and hike through searing heat just to find a box of trinkets."[18]

One spring event near Des Moines, Iowa, even pitted GPS–wielding kids against one another in a race to track down hidden caches of Easter eggs.[19]

Tech-savvy Londoners, meanwhile, have taken to another, more advanced wireless game. Combining PDAs, the Internet, and their vast metropolis, young adventures routinely compete against one another in an adventure called "Uncle Roy All Around You." As first reported by the BBC, up to twelve street participants start out from a central location, using their PDAs to help them find Uncle Roy, who supplies them with clues about his whereabouts.

Over the course of an hour, players spread out, exploring parts of the city they might never otherwise visit, and interacting with people they've never met, in their quest to find Uncle Roy. Meanwhile, the street players' teammates, accessing a virtual map of the city online, help guide the real-world players to various destinations that might include Uncle Roy's hideout.

Online players can communicate with street players via text messaging, and those on the ground can leave voice messages for their online teammates.

"All the reference points that come through to look out for are things you would not notice [just] walking through that part of the city," Catherine Williams, development officer for Blast Theory, the group that runs the game, told BBC News. "It can be a very powerful or very profound experience."[20]

What It Means to Marketers

Geocaching and other virtual/real-world mobile games are natural fits for outdoor and adventure brands. Recreational equipment retailer REI, for instance, is a sponsor for geocaching.com. Navigational device manufacturer Magellan has hosted its own geocaching contests. And, not surprisingly, DaimlerChrysler's Jeep consumer brand is among the first major brands to embrace the trend.

In a promotion called "Jeep 4x4 Cache-In Adventure," the company hosted a nationwide geocaching game that found participants searching for each of 4,000 Jeep 4x4 Travel Bugs hidden in locations around the nation. Each Travel Bug consisted of a yellow die-cast Jeep Wrangler with an official tag attached. Contestants could use a code listed on the tag to log on to an exclusive Web page and find directions to more Travel Bugs, and the chance to win one of three new Jeep 4x4s. Contestants sent in images taken from their camera phones and posted comments as they made their way to each cache—some complaining that other contestants had indeed pilfered many of the Travel Bugs.

Many other brands are tapping into the trend. Toyota's youth-oriented Scion brand, for instance, launched the ScionSpy contest to enable participants to use camera phones or digital cameras to capture and post images of Scions at scionspy.com for the chance to win home theater equipment.

Look for more brands to embrace mobility as a gaming mechanism. Wireless phone carrier Verizon has been promoting this possibility with its own Urban Challenge on Campus promotion, which pits teams of contestants against each other in a race to go to as many checkpoints on college campuses in order to snap an image of the team at each location, and then make it back to the starting point within ninety minutes.

Likewise, London's Chrysalis radio network uses MMS contests to get listeners to send in camera phone images of say, the worst haircut they see today, for the chance to win prizes.

"Part of the activity is to build a database, so they can send later promotions, quizzes, and information where third-party advertisers are able to communicate with consumers," says Carsten Boers, CEO of London-based Flytxt, one of many mobile solutions firms behind such efforts.

In the future, the same kind of promotions can be deployed in intelligent, connected retail environments that reward shoppers for trying certain products or visiting certain departments or stores.

THE WIRELESS UNDERGROUND

Perhaps the most, um, interesting mobile social phenomena at mid-decade: "Bluejacking," and its more lascivious cousin, "Toothing."

Bluetooth, you'll remember, is technology built into devices—handset to wireless earpiece, or PC to wireless keyboard, for instance—that allow them to communicate wirelessly within thirty feet of one another. When set to "on," Bluetooth automatically identifies the Bluetooth devices nearby.

Using a cell phone with Bluetooth, a "Bluejacker" can create a phonebook contact with a prank message, "I really like that skimpy dress!" in the name field. When they hit search, the phone searches for other Bluetooth phones to connect with. Once one or more devices are found, the Bluejacker hits send and the message appears on the "victim's" phone. The victim, of course, has no idea how the message appeared, or who sent it—which apparently is great fun for the Bluejacker. One common trick is to use a camera phone to snap a picture of the confused victim trying to figure how they received the message. A second message with the image of the victim is usually enough to really get attention.

Most of the time, this is just mischievous. Sometimes, it's a fun way to flirt, as long as both parties are game. Sometimes, it's called Toothing.

According to various reports, Toothing involves strangers in restaurants, supermarkets, trains, or buses, using their Bluetooth-enabled cell phones to solicit anonymous sex. "Anyone Toothing?" is a typical missive sent randomly on a bus, bar, or a restaurant.[21]

Apparently, half the fun is discovering who has a Bluetooth phone, and who of those is willing to bite. If another party is interested, messages are exchanged until a suitable location is arranged. As the craze has caught on, participants have wisely taken more time to ascertain the other party's gender, as well as their sexual preferences and proclivities.

What It Means to Marketers

Amazingly, a survey of 500 cell phone users from London-based public relations firm Ranier PR found that 74 percent of respondents said they were interested in receiving short-range, location-based promotional information via such technologies as Bluetooth.[22]

"There is clearly an opportunity for savvy marketers to use this channel," Ranier managing director Stephen Waddington said in a statement to *ZDNet UK*. But he cautioned not to take the opportunity as "a green light." That last part is excellent advice. Most people have no idea what Bluejacking is, and when they find out, they won't be happy.

As far as Toothing's concerned, well, that's your own business.

"There's probably not a lot of opportunity there," jokes Jupiter's Laszlo. "Unless, of course, you're Trojan condoms."

Q & A

Photo: Robin Good

Howard Rheingold:
The Mobile Net's New "Mob" Mentality

Howard Rheingold knows a revolution when he sees one. In 1993, he wrote *The Virtual Community* before most people had ever even ventured onto the Internet. And in his landmark book *Smart Mobs: The Next Social Revolution*, he explored the outer fringes of the mobile Web, and how it's creating new bonds between human beings—for better and for worse.

Writing for the online tech community *The Feature*, and his *Smart Mobs* blog, Rheingold continues this exploration of how mobile technologies are reshaping the social, political, and economic landscape worldwide. He says smart mobs represent a fundamentally new form of social connectivity that will empower the "mobile many" to have fun and do both good and evil in the decade ahead.

RICK MATHIESON: Why makes smart mobbing such a powerful social force?

HOWARD RHEINGOLD: People all over the world are beginning to discover that they can use coordinative technologies—the mobile phone, the Internet—to coordinate face-to-face activities. On the more privileged social side of the spectrum, we have the "flash mob" phenomenon. A lot of people say, well, 'Geez, there's no purpose for that.' I say,

'What's the purpose of standing in line buying a ticket and sitting in a stadium with 100,000 people to watch men in tight pants kick a ball around?' It's entertainment. What's interesting about flash mobs is that it's self-organized entertainment. You're not standing in line buying a ticket and having someone else's prepackaged entertainment sent to you.

At the other end of the spectrum, we have the president of Korea elected by a combination of a "citizen reporter" Web site, AllmyNews.com, and people using e-mail and text messages to coordinate get-out-the-vote efforts. When they put a call out literally during the election that their candidate was losing in the exit polls, they got out to vote and hit that election. In Spain, there was the terrorist bombing, and the elections several days later, in which there were official government-organized demonstrations followed by self-organized demonstrations. They were organized by SMS and may well have tipped that election.

And in the United States, we saw the [Howard] Dean [presidential] campaign using his blog and Meetup.com to organize. At one point he was bringing in $50,000 a day in small contributions, and 140,000 people at house parties were actively promoting him. And although Dean did not get the [nomination], this ultimately is going to change the way politics is run in the Unites States.

So, clearly something is happening worldwide; it's at the level of many people organizing some urban entertainment. And it's at the level of deciding who's going to be president of a country. And that threshold for collective action is lowered by the merger of the mobile telephone, the PC, and the Internet.

RM: How will the next wave of multimedia, mobile broadband networks, and location-aware technologies impact the dynamics of smart mobbing?

HR: Hiptop Nation is the first example of something that can evolve. Hiptop Nation is a combination of picture phones and blogging—people sending small, low-res photographs and a few words from their wireless device through a Web site. And that will evolve as these new technologies evolve.

Moblogging is a really interesting example of people, spread out all over the world, using mobile devices and the Web to get information out. It may seem frivolous, but it illustrates how mobile technologies can change how we view time, the way we navigate our cities, and how we collaborate with other groups of people. I think both blogging and picture phones are very powerful phenomena in themselves, but when you combine the ability of anyone on the street to send media from where they are to anyone else in the world through the Web, I think it portends significant changes, though it's rudimentary today.

Add in GPS [and other] location capabilities that let you know where your buddies are, or how to get wherever it is you're going, and that will enhance this revolution significantly.

And, in connection with that, the ability to add presence [awareness], presence being like your buddy list on Instant Messenger, so you know who is in the neighborhood now, will be huge. We're seeing some experiments with that, not necessarily from the big companies, but from small experimenters like Dodgeball. So, that's going to make a huge difference. It's hard to tell at this point whether this is going to grow from grassroots efforts like Dodgeball, or whether some [cellular service carriers] are going to get the clue and start offering that, too.

RM: What does this all mean for marketers?

HR: Anybody that has bought anything on eBay knows how reputation systems work. Before you buy something, you want to know whether to trust the seller. Online, mobile or otherwise, you can go find out what people who have bought things from that person before are saying.

Imagine the whole notion of information on places: location blogging where you subscribe to a group or service to see what kind of information they have on real places, 'This restaurant is no good,' or, 'This is my favorite bookstore.' One of the first applications I've seen is for speed traps. Someone notices a speed trap, and then sends a notice, or it pops up on [an online] map, for everyone else to see. I'm sure that law enforcement is not happy about that, but that's an example of the kinds of things that people come up with.

Likewise, the manufacturers of mass products are not going to be able to hide for very long if people are talking amongst each other about them.

Which brings me to yet another aspect of this, which is being able to use your mobile device to point at the bar code or RFID tag on a manufactured product and find out all kinds of things—from what kinds of ingredients are in there that aren't on the label, or a Webcam at the factory where teenagers are assembling your sneakers in Pakistan, or what either the Moral Majority or the ACLU has to say about the politics of this company. That could tip power to consumers and clear the way for the kind of economic smart mobbing that would create very significant changes, if that happens.

A friend of mine who's a Microsoft researcher has put together a handheld wireless device with a bar code reader and connected it to Google.

I was able to go into his kitchen, scan a box of prunes, and see that it was distributed by the Sun-Diamond Growers Cooperative. You Google Sun-Diamond, and you find "U.S. versus Sun-Diamond," [an article] on the U.S. Supreme Court looking at questionable lobbying practices. You will see a partisan site called corpwatch.org with their headline to the effect of "Bromide Barons Suppress Democratic Process." You're not going to find this out in the label, but Sun-Diamond is [allegedly] the largest contributor to lobbying against control of the chemical methyl bromide.

Sun-Diamond is not going to tell you that. But if you Google it, if you connect that ability to find that information out there to your ability to scan something in real time, that changes a lot.

RM: So how can companies embrace smart mobs and use them to have a positive impact on their business?

HR: Any business that can't keep in touch with business makers, key people, and customers when they need to is going to fall behind. We're seeing that people who can't be interrupted by phone calls can be reached by SMS or instant messaging, and that groups are able to coordinate their activities at all times anywhere around the globe.

When your buddy list is an executive team or an engineering team that is split up around the world, to react to the conditions very quickly, being able to not just talk, but know when the others are online, send them text, send them rich messages, and send them documents, in real time, is pretty important. And it will make all the difference in a competitive situation.

From a marketing perspective, I think this is the very opposite of some small group deciding who's going to be marketed to. Many communities are, for the most part, self-organized. So, I think you're not going to get that smart mob power unless you have something that really moves a lot of people to go out and self-organize. It's like how AOL tried to build a top-down Internet with their little 'walled garden' of Web sites. That's not the same as having millions of people put up their own Web pages and link to each other, and create 4 billion Web pages in 2,000 days. It's about harnessing the power of collective action that enables anybody to act in a way that adds up, not organizing something from the top down and trying to broadcast it. There are some things you just can't do that way.

CHAPTER EIGHT

Marketing 2020

The Future According to Spielberg

A decade from now, marketing book gurus will write about how the wireless era was really just a prelude to whatever comes next; chapter two of the Internet's ongoing storyline.

Much of what we predict today will prove dead wrong or morph into directions hardly dreamed of.

From our perch in the second half of the first decade of the twenty-first century, we can look back ten years, to the birth of Amazon.com in 1994, and eBay and Yahoo in 1995, followed by a myriad of consumer and business Web sites accessed via something called a Web browser and a mind-numbingly slow 14.4-kbs modem.

Looking forward ten years, what do we see?

Is it a world like *There*, where we browse the wireless Internet from sunglasses? Will the convergence of a high-speed, global wireless Web, XML, GPS, RFID, Wi-Fi, and other technologies, combined with fuel cell–powered mobile devices, create a truly "pervasive" or "ubiquitous" global network that proactively delivers services based on our individual preferences? Instead of working the Net to get what we want, will the Internet finally work for us, delivering whatever we want, whenever we want, wherever we want it?

As evidenced by numerous examples in this book, many technology experts seem to think so.

"The big change is going to be when the Internet follows you, not you trying to follow the Internet," is how Motorola CEO Ed Zander recently put it to *USA Today*. "It's just there. Your life is just affected the way it's affected today by the lights in a room."[1]

To hear many experts tell it, the Net will feature pervasive services that work seamlessly online and off, wireline and wirelessly. And most prognosticators offer some variation on Kenny Hirschorn's prediction that ten to fifteen years from now, services deployed over a pervasive, global, always-on Internet will wake you up in the morning, read you your e-mail, schedule and reschedule your day based on traffic patterns, your travel plans, or unexpected meetings, buy plane tickets, buy a gift for your upcoming wedding anniversary, and direct your call to a conference venue. You'll call up news, entertainment, or shopping content anywhere, anytime. And your entire day will be recorded, TiVo style, so you can relive moments however and whenever you want.

According to a study from telecommunications firm Ericsson, consumers aren't interested in these technologies in and of themselves. They're interested in solutions that make their lives easier and help them do the things they already do easier and faster, whether it's staying in touch with friends, capturing life's moments, listening to music, or playing games.[2]

"People really don't want to buy technology," says Lisa Hook, head of America Online's broadband unit, which is busy extending AOL e-mail, messaging, photos, news, and other properties into the wireless frontier. "They want to buy experiences. . . . We want users to be able to create an ecosystem of devices and put the AOL experiences on them"[3]

REPORT FROM TOMORROW

We've talked a lot about such future possibilities in this book. But what does it all mean for marketers over the long, long term?

Ironically, to get one of the more compelling—and perhaps most realistic—views of marketing a decade from now, you have to go back to the future, to the year 2002, when Oscar-winning filmmaker Steven Spielberg released a noir-ish sci-fi thriller called *Minority Report.*

Those who have seen the film know *Report* ostensibly depicts the world of 2054, and casts Tom Cruise as John Anderton, the head of the District of Columbia's Department of Pre-Crime, which uses precognitive humans, called "pre-cogs," to predict murders before they happen.

Based on a 1956 short story by Philip K. Dick, the movie is unabashedly didactic. But it conjures up enough third-act plot twists and wicked-cool action scenes to keep things sufficiently interesting.

Still, what makes the film captivating isn't its plot, but its pre-science. In a feat of creative and technological genius, the filmmaker immerses viewers in a consumer-driven world of ubiquitous computing, supposedly at least fifty years hence.

"Steven wanted to portray a future that was based around a familiar, market-based western society in approximately fifty years time," says Alex McDowell, the film's production designer. So McDowell used input from a three-day think tank Spielberg held to gather insights from twenty-three top futurists.

"The goal was to create a realistic view of a plausible future," says Peter Schwartz, the head of the *Minority Report* think tank, and chairman of Global Business Network, a consultancy based in Emeryville, California.

The problem: The scenarios the futurists presented to reflect 2054 were too unbelievable—including organic buildings that grow and change according to the needs of occupants; "cancer bombs," implanted at birth, that deploy microscopic robots to destroy cancer cells as they develop later in life; people embedded with bionic cell phones and computing devices; and biomechanical automobiles that put a new spin on our proclivity to anthropomorphize our cars.

"Quite quickly, Steven said it's too fantastical, even if it may be true," says McDowell. "He didn't want the audience to doubt the content of the film, or to consider it to be fantasy. It was really important that it was rooted in a reality."

So the team took aim not at 2054, but more like 2020. Projecting out from today's marketing and media technologies—Web cookies, GPS devices, cell phones, TiVo personal video recorders, RFID, and more—the filmmakers gave shape to an advertising-saturated society where billboards call out to you on a first-name basis. Paper newspapers deliver continuously updated news over a broadband wireless network. Holographic hosts greet you at retail stores where biometric retina scans deduct the cost of goods from your bank account. And cereal boxes broadcast animated commercials.

"We set off in a direction of a wirelessly networked, ubiquitously connected urban environment," says McDowell. "We looked at trends in mass-market culture in place today, and took them to their limit—creating a world where omnipresent, one-to-one advertising recognizes you, and sells directly to you as an individual."

Starting to sound familiar?

Amazingly, the technologies portrayed in the film aren't even close to being science fiction; you've been reading about some of their predecessors in this book. In fact, many of these marketing tools are currently in development. And they're coming much sooner than you think.

NEWS FLASH

In the film, *USA Today* and other newspapers and magazines stream news updates, right before your eyes, with ink moving around and rearranging itself on the page, based on incoming, wirelessly transmitted information.

In the real world, this is one possible extension of new "digital paper" technologies currently being developed by companies with names like E-Ink, magink, and Gyricon.

We're not talking tablet PCs here, but paper, or something very close to it, that can receive updates over a wireless network and can be folded under your arm, slipped into a briefcase, or used to line a birdcage.

"You'll start to see these things in the next ten to fifteen years," says Russ Wilcox, general manager and cofounder of E-Ink, based in Cambridge, Massachusetts.[4]

Called "electronic ink," the technology uses electricity to move microcapsules of pigmentation painted on paper-thin plastic to create moving images. Today, Wilcox's company is working on new technology that will be able to print cheap transistors, and, someday, tiny antennas, directly into the "paper"—making it a receiver for displaying images and sounds.

"The idea is a computer display that looks and feels just like a newspaper but has a little receiver built into it," says Wilcox. "It would receive wireless updates so you always have a newspaper that's up to date."

The same technologies could enable cereal boxes to play television commercials, like the "Pine & Oats" packaging in *Minority Report* that broadcasts animated characters singing the product's theme song, complete with the latest promotional offer.

Early forms of digital ink technology are in use worldwide. E-Ink's technology is in use in the Sony Librié, an electronic book reader that is about the same size and weight as a slim paperback.[5] And magink, a company based in New York City, creates a product that is used in Japan on almost 1,000 high-resolution, full-color digital signs and billboards.[6] In magink's case, reflective, oily organic paste is set between two conductive glass or plastic plates. The sign retains its color until it receives a new electrical signal to change again. The signs, which also happen to be solar-powered, can even be updated wirelessly to display changing weather, ads, or traffic information.

"Digital technology in general is going to change the face of outdoor advertising," magink CEO Ran Poliakine recently told *Wired* magazine, adding that the technology could even be embedded in products all around us. "You can cover your living room with digital wallpaper that will be able to change, even the color, according to the seasons around the year," he said. "The technology promises a real change in the way people receive information."[7]

A WORLD (WIDE WEB) AT YOUR FINGERTIPS

This same technology also provides another key component of *Report*, which is the idea that one day, you will be able to pull up information and utilities as you want them, from a vast wireless network. Our hero Anderton, for instance, is able to call up information, projected on any nearby wall, or even in midair, and then use hand gestures to get the information he needs.

As we've learned in this book, the idea of accessing content and projecting it via wireless networks is already increasingly commonplace.

McDowell and his team took it one step further. "[What] we wanted to establish was that your environment was essentially intelligent and that walls could be coated with a kind of LCD–like material that was very inexpensive," says McDowell. "So it's essentially like digital wallpaper that could both transmit and receive, and that glass would be embedded with sort of intelligence so it has the ability to transmit data as well. We established that these intelligent surfaces could receive data and could engage in gesture recognition."

Indeed, this interface wouldn't be driven by cell phones or Dertouzos-ian sunglasses, but rather by high-tech gloves that are used to manipulate the interface.

Inspired by the gestures scientists used to communicate with alien beings in Spielberg's *Close Encounters of the Third Kind*, McDowell and his team worked with MIT professor John Underkoffler to develop a gesture recognition language for interfacing with the computer.

"John developed a coherent language that was believable because [Tom Cruise's character] was using gestures that had specific meaning based on the lexicon Underkoffler had developed," says McDowell.

LIFE AS A POP-UP AD

Meanwhile, today's GPS and wireless network technologies may lead to the place-based, personalized advertising that provides a backdrop for the film's city scenes.

In *Minority Report*, retina scanners monitor subway passengers and automatically collect their fare. Posters, billboards, and gonfalons talk directly to individual consumers.

At one point, after Anderton pays a black-market surgeon to replace his eyeballs with someone else's in order to avoid being tracked by police, a holographic greeter "reads" those eyes and cheerfully exclaims, "Hello Mr. Yakimoto, welcome back to the Gap. How did those assorted tank tops work out?"

"We're clearly moving in this direction in all forms of marketing already," says Schwartz. "The infrastructure behind identifying and mapping an individual's preference, consumer behavior, history, and so on is in its most primitive forms on the Web today. We leave a trace of our activities and presence in a variety of ways, and software out there is sensing us and responding immediately to who we are, particularly with respect to retail offerings."

Technology is extending this scenario into real-world advertising displays. Today, for instance, technology called Human Locator, from Canadian ad agency Freeset Interactive, detects when humans are near, tracks their movement, and then broadcasts messages directed at them from a nearby screen.[8] It's not a huge stretch to imagine the technology wirelessly tying some form of personal identification to back-end databases in order to call up relevant offers based on personal buying behavior. From there, such a system could easily be augmented with transaction capabilities.

Of course, it's unclear whether we're really talking about machines that read our retinas in order to establish identity, much less to conduct transactions. But it's a possibility: Many states already use facial recognition and other "biometric" systems to search for individuals who have obtained multiple driver's licenses by lying about their identity. According to the *New York Times*, the police department of Pinellas County, Florida, recently began deploying one such system in police cars so officers can check the people they stop against a database of photographs.[9]

But experts believe retina scans used to identify individuals for commercial purposes is indeed fifty years away. In the shorter term, personalized transactions will likely be enabled by other wireless technologies.

One possibility is fingerprinting. Today, police in Portland, Oregon, and other cities use mobile devices to scan a person's fingerprints and compare them with other fingerprints in a database.[10] Why not just place your fingerprint on a screen to have offers presented and transactions conducted, with no possibility for fraud or identity theft?

Disney World has been using fingerprint scanners to identify annual and seasonal pass holders since 1996. Paper-based passes have names and expirations on the front, and a magnetic strip containing your biometric finger scan, which it compares to your fingers when you swipe them through a device at the entry gate.[11] According to one study from the U.S. Bureau of Justice Statistics and think tank Privacy and American Business found that 85 percent of consumers feel biometric finger imaging would be perfectly acceptable for many transactions, including verifying the identity of customers making credit card purchases.[12]

A more fantastic possibility: Computer chips, embedded underneath the skin, could conceivably enable such transactions. Ottawa-based Zarlink Semiconductor is developing body area networks based on implanted medical chips that enable doctors to monitor and adjust pacemakers and hearing aids wirelessly.[13] There's no reason these and other wireless technologies can't be transferred to the retail world and tied to backend transactional databases.

But while many security and identification technologies like these originate from research and early implementations related to military and police operations, the business world has its own route to highly personalized—and less invasive—interactions with consumers.

Instead, RFID tags, miniature sensors, and other technologies could easily be embedded in credit cards, watches, cell phones, or jewelry, or some other wireless transceiver device, to quickly scan a person for identity and then access backend databases to best suit the individual's needs.

"I don't think there will be any one answer," says Schwartz. "Some merchants will go one way, some individuals may go another. Today, when I go to the checkout stand at the supermarket, is it my credit card, is it cash, is it check, is it my ATM card? I can choose my mode of transaction. For a long time, there will be a multiplicity of transaction modes."

Of course, as cool as wireless technologies can be, the real heavy lifting will come from those back-end databases, tied together in massive, integrated networks, as companies, and the conglomerates behind them, try to serve consumers in amazing new ways.

One early, experimental form of this has been under development by the Transportation Security Administration (TSA) as part of proposed enhancements to the national Computer-Aided Passenger Pre-Screening (CAPPS) system used at airports.

The original CAPPS system was designed to collect and store basic travel information whether you bought your ticket with cash or credit card, whether you're a frequent flier, and when was the last time you flew. But the system had serious flaws. The September 11 terrorists, for instance, outsmarted CAPPS by conducting test runs to determine whether a specific hijacker would be identified as a potential threat—and then replaced those who raised suspicions.

In response, the federal government set out to develop CAPPS II. Sanctioned by provisions of the USA Patriot Act, CAPPS II was designed to use extensive data mining and analysis tools to access information spanning a nationwide "Information Power Grid" made up of consumer and government databases. The idea was to quickly render a complete picture of an individual traveler and then run algorithms to assess threat risk.

The system, set for initial rollout by the end of 2005, was

dropped, for now at least, in favor of a modified version, called Secure Flights, that uses less extensive measures—not so much over privacy concerns, but over the practicality of rolling out such a massive system in such a short time frame.

Meanwhile, GPS and other location-based technologies are already used to target ads to users in specific locations. New Wi-Fi–based location-enabled networks (LENs) can carve up a wireless network into discrete segments that target users passing through a specified location. And other avenues for consumer targeting are on the way.

The FCC's "E911" mandate dictates that all new cell phone handsets must include GPS that pinpoints the location of owners in the event they dial 911. Once in place, it could be just a matter of time before marketers find ways to serve up offers based on user location.

In fact, all that data could be stored in databases to build profiles on each individual consumer, so services could not just respond to requests, but recommend products and services like some real-world version of Amazon's book recommendation feature.

The foundation for such database systems is being built by companies such as Axciom and ChoicePoint, which collect massive amounts of information on hundreds of millions of people—names, addresses, Social Security numbers, license and deed transfers, motor vehicle registrations, and more. Today, this sort of data is collected, packaged, and sold mostly without consumer knowledge—a painful point of contention in 2005 when a ring of suspected identity thieves fraudulently obtained personal information on over 145,000 U.S. consumers from Atlanta-based ChoicePoint.[14]

What's more, many wrinkles will need to be worked out before networks of interconnected databases gain widespread consumer appeal. Nearly 1,000 innocent airline travelers, for instance, have found themselves on airline security watch lists by mistake—mysteriously ID'd by back-end databases as security threats and required to go through intense security administration questioning every time they try to board airplanes—with no real understanding of how to clear their good names.[15] Just think what will happen when those kinds of errors are propagated across innumerable business databases around the globe. Today, nobody really knows what kind of safeguards and limitations will be in place to protect consumers, and what kind of recourse consumers will have when errors are made.

MARKETING NIRVANA, OR PRIVACY NIGHTMARE?

Right about now, you may be thinking, hold on a sec. How did we go from talking about some really cool marketing technologies to something that's starting to sound irritating at best, and scary at worst? What happens if I don't want to be wirelessly tracked, targeted, and tied to some worldwide network of databases?

Technology, of course, is always a double-edged sword. As a movie, *Minority Report* isn't a dream scenario; it's an action thriller set in an Orwellian dystopia. And the sorts of futuristic applications I've described help the movie tell a cautionary tale about one possible trajectory of today's rampant consumerism: the creation of a stratified, mass-mediated society where the rich actually pay to avoid advertising, and where wireless network- and biometrics-enabled marketing displays incessantly pitch product to a hapless proletariat.

In the film, the upper class lives in a historically protected environment and is not visibly advertised to, because they can afford not to be. The second strata is comprised of the nouveau riche and upper urban society who live in a kind of mall city, where they have access to enormous amounts of interactive material, which brings with it a large amount of advertising. "If you want the best latest cereal, you're going to get this jingle annoyingly going off in your ear," says McDowell. "And if you go to the mall, you're going to be advertised to whether you like it or not."

And what about that third strata—the working class? "The people with the least money are being advertised to the most," says McDowell. "And that seems to have some kind of a logic based on the way things are going now."

Indeed, for all their commercial potential, looking at the possible future of today's wireless technologies against the tableau of a movie like *Minority Report* makes it clear that these tools are not devoid of ethical considerations.

"A world in which you are connected infinitely is a world in which you are also surveilled infinitely," warns techno anthropologist Howard Rheingold.[16] "Since we have both the political infrastructure and the technological capability for the state to spy on just about everybody at all times, this is something that we should deliberate carefully before it can become a fact."

And we had better hurry. The same technological concepts behind CAPPS II also drove the Bush administration's dream for a "Total Information Awareness" system, which, as originally conceived, would create a vast global electronic dragnet that would sift through every person's personal histories—all online and offline purchases, medical records, online activities, and communications, and other data—and then use statistical techniques to identify suspicious patterns in an attempt to apprehend terrorists before they strike.[17] Consulting firm Booz Allen Hamilton was awarded $1.5 million worth of work on what was originally conceived as a $62.9 million project to get the first TIA systems in place by 2007.[18]

The program, later rechristened "Terrorist Information Awareness," has supposedly been shelved at the urging of privacy advocates and some members of Congress. Nonetheless, the basic building blocks for such a system are no doubt being developed today. Schwartz believes that the project has simply gone classified.

But there are other troubling developments. Aligo, a company based in Mountain View, California, offer products that help employers track their field teams' movements with GPS–based cell phones.[19]

Officials in Chicago and New York have begun implementing massive surveillance efforts with cameras placed throughout their respective cities. By the end of 2006, Chicago, for instance, plans to have 2,250 "smart cameras" set up around the city—making Chicagoans some of the most closely watched in the world. The technology is designed to recognize suspicious activities around buildings considered terrorist targets—people dropping off packages and walking away, people wandering aimlessly, or cars pulling along-side the freeway—all monitored so police can dispatch officers to potential trouble spots in some real-world version of Sim City.[20] According to Schwartz, virtually every American is already now captured by surveillance cameras an average of thirty-eight times per day.

Combined with solutions like those used to secure the 2004 Olympics, many new surveillance cameras like those from San Diego–based Science Applications International Corp. (SAIC) are able to collect spoken words with speech-recognition software to transcribe text and then search for patterns along with other electronic communications to identify security risks.[21]

Even the human mind may not be entirely off limits. According to documents released to the Electronic Privacy Information Center under the Freedom of Information Act, NASA has worked with an undisclosed commercial partner to explore the possibility of developing something called "noninvasive neuroelectric sensors." According to the documents, the sensors would be designed to be embedded in airport security stations and wirelessly monitor brain-wave and heartbeat patterns "to detect passengers who potentially might pose a threat."

Although purely theoretical—NASA says it never seriously considered the research project—it is technically not beyond the realm of possibility. Functional magnetic resonance imaging (fMRI) technologies, for example, easily identify the differences in brainwave patterns when people tell the truth versus when they fib. In fact, stealing a page from the psychic detective "pre-cogs" in *Report*, the technology might one day be able to identify neuroelectric patterns associated with the way the brain functions when a person is planning to commit a crime.

Already, scientists have been experimenting with the technology for commercial purposes. Baylor University scientists used brain scans to determine preference for Coke or Pepsi. Daimler-Chrysler has reportedly used imaging technology to gauge interest in different makes of cars. And scientists at UCLA have been conducting experiments to discover the differences between the brains of Republicans and Democrats.[22]

In the distant future, this kind of technology could conceivably correlate physiologic patterns with computerized data on travel routines, criminal background, and credit information and shopping habits from potentially thousands of databases—giving new meaning to the term "pervasive computing."

Of course, we don't have anything to fear if we don't have anything to hide, as the saying goes. But the prospect of having your brainwaves analyzed, processed, and cross-referenced with data about your family, friends, product preferences, and personal history underscores the tremendous ethical considerations of a society where you can run, but never truly hide.

So what happens when your ability to access any company, content, or service anywhere, anytime, means they—and the government—also have access to you?

"Andy Warhol talked about everyone getting fifteen minutes of fame," says Schwartz. "If we're not careful, everyone may end up with fifteen minutes of privacy.

"The industry will need to create ways for people to opt in or out of these services," he adds. "As a society, we'll have to make a set of judgments about not gathering information about people in a routine way."

Throughout this book, we've talked about the all-important ability for consumers to choose their level of interaction with—and exposure to—promotional overtures, to opt in or out of marketing programs. It is the golden rule of marketing, mobile or otherwise.

Yet anyone who's ever tried to opt out of, say, their financial institution's unheralded programs for sharing personal information with other affiliates or companies, or a marketer's supposedly opt-in e-mail promotions, knows that may be wishful thinking.

Steven Levy, technology columnist for *Newsweek*, believes consumers will grow accepting to these technologies because "the benefits will be immediately apparent, while the privacy drawbacks emerge gradually." He says wireless buddy lists and other electronic "friend finders" will make life more efficient and pleasurable—but that personal and locational information will one day give pause when everything we do will be imminently traceable.

"If nothing is done," he writes, "our love affair with wireless will result in the loss of a hitherto unheralded freedom—the license to get lost."[23]

"We are moving into a transparent society," says Schwartz. "The end of privacy is inevitable. As long as people have the choice of knowing what's going on and buying it or not buying it—the ability to say, 'I refuse to let you have or use information about me,' or 'I don't want to use your service if it requires me to provide certain information'—then it's a matter of choice."

FUTURE SHOCK

With such insights, Spielberg, Schwartz, McDowell, and the rest of the great minds behind *Minority Report* could qualify as pre-cogs themselves. Indeed, if there's anything that makes the film especially prescient, it's the timing.

Though the movie was filmed well before September 11th, its riff on proactively stopping crime before it happens is strangely analogous to the "doctrine of preemption," our government's policy to preemptively strike against terrorists.

And while the technologies shown in *Minority Report* may not all find their way into commercial applications anytime soon, the world of ubiquitous computing has already arrived. And society—not to mention marketers—have a responsibility to make decisions about their deployment and use carefully.

"After 9-11, we have a real trade-off to make," says Schwartz. "Many people are expecting the government to detect destructive forces, but there will be a societal cost. My view of the need for privacy may be different than [former attorney general] John Ashcroft's."

THE POWER BELONGS TO YOU

For all the dangers of the wireless age, says McDowell, the debate over the future is what good science fiction is all about.

"The thing about this genre is that it provides an opportunity to hold a mirror up to the future and extrapolate from things that are happening now in terms of advertising, and the loss of civil liberties, and bring them to their logical or illogical extremes," he says. "It lets us see where things might go, and either steer things in that direction—or steer them completely away."

As marketers (and consumers), you and I will help make that choice. Consumer backlash will no doubt thwart many misuses of the technology, and regrettably, government regulation will be required to stem others.

As we've discussed throughout this book, mBranding can be a tremendously powerful way to enhance the way consumers interact with, and experience, the brands they know and trust. But that last word—trust—is indeed the operative word. The more we create compelling experiences that earn our customers' trust and respect, the more success we will find as the wireless age progresses. mBranding is about brands empowering people to enhance the way they live, work, learn, and play. It is not the subjugation of consumer interests to meet our own profit goals.

The dire predictions made by prognosticators like Spielberg and company—and movies such as *Minority Report*—are not fait accompli, and they certainly should not frighten us. Instead, they should inspire us to make the right choices for both business and society.

In other words, keeping the wireless world safe for both commerce and liberty means we must heed the warnings of the precogs already among us.

Notes

INTRODUCTION

1. Mid-2005 projection, based on a report by Brad Stone, "Your Next Computer," *Newsweek*, June 7, 2004, p. 51; IDC, "Worldwide Mobile Phone 2004–2008 Forecast and Analysis," April 2004; Yankee Group: estimates, June 16, 2004.
2. In-Stat/MDR, "Event Horizon: Two Billion Mobile Subscribers by 2007, 2003 Subscriber Forecast," August 6, 2003.
3. Palm computing aficionado Jim Thompson, "Palm Power: On the Computing Power of the Palm Pilot," 1997, http://www .jimthompson.net/palmpda/Silly/power.htm.
4. Estimate, based on total number of 150 million wireless laptops worldwide by 2005 (In-Stat MDR, Nokia, and Gartner Dataquest Stand, 2001: 6 million tablet PCs and 8.4 million smart phones; Datamonitor estimate of 2005 handheld penetration: 510 million (many, but not all, wireless-enabled).
5. *Business Week*, "The Info Tech 100," June 21, 2004, p. 74.
6. *CNETAsia*, "Korea to Invest US$1.7bn in Smart Homes," May

16, 2003, http://asia.cnet.com/news/personaltech/0,39037091, 39130965,00.htm.

7. The *New York Times Magazine*, December 14, 2003, p. 93.

8. Enpocket, "Mobile Media Monitor," May 18, 2004.

9. AT&T Wireless estimates.

10. IDC estimates.

11. Lori Valigra, "Fabricating the Future," *Christian Science Monitor*, August 29, 2002.

12. Megan Scully, "Tiny Sentinels," *Defense News*, January 20, 2004.

13. Pew Internet & American Life Project, "The Broadband Difference: How Online Americans' Behavior Changes with High-Speed Internet Connections at Home," June 22, 2002.

14. Nielsen Media Research, "Research Paper: Men 18–34 Prime-time Television Study," November 2003.

15. Associated Press, "Box Office Receipts Soar to Record in '04," January 3, 2005.

16. Veronis Suhler Stevenson, as reported by Kevin J. Delaney, "Ads in Videogames Pose a New Threat to Media Industry," the *Wall Street Journal*, July 28, 2004.

17. Entertainment Software Association, "Essential Facts, 2004," May 2004, www.theesa.com/EFBrochure.pdf.

18. Yankee Group, "U.S. Mobile Entertainment Survey," July 1, 2004.

19. Nat Ives, "All Commercials, All the Time," *New York Times*, July 26, 2004.

20. Yankee Group statement, "Yankee Group Forecast Shows 33.5 Million DVR Homes by End of 2008," December 16, 2004, http://www.itfacts.biz/index.php?id = P1969.

21. Stefanie Olsen, "Google-like Technologies Could Revolutionize TV, Other Media," *CNET News*, April 29, 2004.

22. Internet Advertising Bureau/PricewaterhouseCoopers, "IAB Internet Advertising Revenue Report, FY 2003," April 2004; mobile advertising projections, Forrester Research Stance, July 2001.

23. Syntegra White Paper, "The Evolution of the Wireless Revolution," 2003, p. 1, www.us.syntegra.com/acrobat/208921.pd.

CHAPTER ONE

1. Horst Hortner, Christopher Lindinger, and others, "Pervasive Information Acquisition for Mobile AR–Navigation Systems," white paper, October 2003, http://www.swe.uni-linz.ac.at/publications/abstract/TR-SE-03.10.html.

2. Kevin Maney, "No Time Off? It's Tech Giants' fault," *USA TODAY*, July 21, 2004.

3. Rick Mathieson, "The Wireless Future Looks Orange," *Mpulse Magazine*, July 2001, http://www.cooltown.com/cooltown/mpulse/0701-hirschhorn.asp.

4. Broadchannel.com, http://www.broadchannel.com/education_glossary.asp.

5. Douglas Heingartner, "Connecting Paper and Online Worlds by Cellphone Camera," *New York Times*, October 7, 2004.

6. Ginny Parker, "NTT DoCoMo's New Handsets Will Double as Commerce Tools," *Wall Street Journal*, June 17, 2004.

7. Consect, "2004 Mobile Music Report," 2004, http://www.consect.com.

8. Reuters, "Ring Tones Bringing in Big Bucks," *Wired News*, January 13, 2004.

9. Rick Mathieson, "Battle of the Network Stars: TV's New Race for Ratings on the Wireless Web," *Mpulse Magazine*, September 2002, http://www.hpbazaar.com/cooltown/mpulse/0902-networktv.asp.

10. Ibid.

11. Kent Wertime, "Involve Me, or Forget Me," *Viewpoint Online Magazine*, http://www.ogilvy.com/viewpoint/view_ko.php?id=41377&imagald=1.

12. Ivy Schmerken, "Wireless-Retail Financial Services: Adoption Can't Justify the Cost," *Wall Street & Technology Online*, August 12, 2002, http://www.wallstreetandtech.com/showArticle.jhtml?articleID=14702792.

13. Rick Mathieson, "Banking on Wireless: The New Economics of Mobile Financial Services," *Mpulse Magazine*, October 2001, http://www.cooltown.com/cooltown/mpulse/1001-financial.asp.

14. "BonFire Media's Innovation on Java Technology Spars eBay Evolution," corporate release.

15. Rick Mathieson, "The Mobility Belle: The Jaclyn Easton Interview," *Mpulse Magazine*, June 2002, http://www.cooltown.com/cooltown/mpulse/0602-easton.asp.

15. Ibid.

CHAPTER TWO

1. Cynthia H. Cho, "For More Advertisers, The Medium Is the Text Message," *Wall Street Journal*, August 2, 2004.

2. Rick Mathieson, "Reach Out & Sell Someone," *Mpulse Magazine*, July 2001, http://www.cooltown.com/cooltown/mpulse/0701-wirelessad.asp.

3. Kate Kaye, "Q2 Ad Serving Findings: Increase in Eye-Catching Ads, Drop in Geo-Targeting," MediaPost, *Media Daily News*, July 27, 2004.

4. Enpocket, "Mobile Media Monitor," July 2004, http://www.enpocket.com/wrapper/page.php?content=news/2004/dec13 us.html.

5. Based on Jupiter research estimates, as cited by Zachary Rodgers, "Mobile Marketing: whr r we now," *ClickZ Network*, June 21, 2004.

6. Nat Ives, "Taking Pictures of Magazine Ads," *New York Times*, August 25, 2004.

7. Cho, op. cit.

8. Mathieson, op. cit.

9. Anita Ramasastry, "Why the New Federal 'CAN Spam' Law Probably Won't Work," *CNN.com*, December 5, 2003, http://www.cnn.com/2003/LAW/12/05/findlaw.analysis.ramasastry.spam/.

10. Tom Zeller Jr., "Law Barring Junk E-Mail Allows a Flood Instead," *New York Times*, February 1, 2005.

11. Thomas Claburn, "Spim, Like Spam, Is on the Rise," *Informa-*

tion Week, March 30, 2004, http://www.informationWeek.com/story/showArticle.jhtml?articleID=18600413.

12. Ibid.

13. Riva Richmond, "Pre-Emptive Strike: Cell Phone Spam Isn't a Huge Problem Yet. And Regulators Want to Make Sure it Never Is," *Wall Street Journal*, September 13, 2004.

14. Catharine P. Taylor, "The Text Files," *ADWEEK*, July 12, 2004, p. 16.

15. Rick Mathieson, "Dunkin for Euros," *Mpulse Magazine*, May 2002, http://www.cooltown.com/cooltown/mpulse/0502-commerce.asp.

16. Enpocket, op. cit.

17. GSM Association, European SMS Guide, January 2003.

18. Forrester Research statement, "Plan, Don't Spam, Forrester Warns Europe's SMS Marketers," January 25, 2002, http://216.239.57.104/search?q=cache:vccN89z9JbcJ:www.fedma.org/img/db/30010 2SMSstudy.pdf+ +Forrester+Warns+Europe%27s+SMS+Marketers%22&hl=en .

19. Roger Park, "Mobile Marketing in 2004," imediaconnection.com, November 4, 2004, http://www.imediaconnection.com/content/4534.asp.

20. Rick Mathieson, "Just for the Text of It: Coca-Cola Launches World's Largest SMS Campaign," *Mpulse Magazine*, August 2003, http://www.hpbazaar.com/cooltown/mpulse/0703-coketxt.asp.

21. Ibid.

22. Lauren Bigaleow, results of SkyGo ad recall study, 2001, as reported by Christopher Saunders, "Skygo: Wireless Ads Work for Branding, Direct Response," *Clickz news*, March 5, 2001, http://www.clickz.com/news/article.php/705101.

23. Solution provider m-Qube release.

24. Rick Mathieson, "Two Thumbs Up: Hollywood's Hit Machine Goes Mobile," *Mpulse Magazine,* October 2003, http://www.cooltown.com/cooltown/mpulse/1003-hitmachine.asp.

25. Sarah Boussofiane, "Sending Your True Feelings: How Can I Say 'I Love You,' 'I Miss You,' 'I'm Sorry'?" *Viewpoint Online Magazine*, May 2004, http://www.ogilvy.com/viewpoint/view_ko.php?id=41380&iMagaId=-1.

26. Rick Mathieson, "Reach Out and Sell Someone," op. cit.

27. Pew Internet & American Life Project, "Consumption of Information Goods and Services in the United States," November 2003.

28. Pew Internet & American Life Project, "28% of American Adults Are Wireless Ready," May 2004, http://www.pewinternet.org/PPF/r/127/report_display.asp.

29. Rick Mathieson, "Two Thumbs Up: Hollywood's Hit Machine Goes Mobile," op. cit.

30. Telephia Report "Online Games Played on Mobile Devices Could Be Key Teen Entertainment Application," corporate release, March 22, 2004.

31. Enpocket, op. cit.

32. Thomas Mucha, "Young and Upwardly Mobile," *Business 2.0*, July 1, 2004, http://www.business2.com/b2/web/articles/0,17863,659808,00.html.

33. Enpocket, op. cit.

34. Ibid.

CHAPTER THREE

1. Rick Mathieson, "Two Thumbs Up: Hollywood's Hit Machine Goes Mobile," *Mpulse Magazine*, October 2003, http://www.cooltown.com/cooltown/mpulse/1003-hitmachine.asp.

2. Ibid.

3. Ibid.

4. Rick Mathieson, "Must See (Mobile) TV? Sprint PCS Brings Digital TV to Cell Phones," *Mpulse Magazine*, January 2004, http://www.hpbazaar.com/cooltown/mpulse/0104-sprinttv.asp.

5. Ginny Parker, "NTT DoCoMo's New Handsets Will Double as Commerce Tools," *Wall Street Journal*, June 17, 2004.

6. Michael Pastore, citing Jupiter projections for 2006, in "Consumers, M-Commerce Fail to Connect," *ClickZ Stats: Wireless*, July 9, 2001.

7. Rick Mathieson, "Reach Out & Sell Someone," *Mpulse Magazine*, July 2001.

8. Juniper statement, "M-Commerce Market to Grow to $40bn Fuelled by Micropayments," May 10, 2004, http://sourcewire .com/releases/rel_display.php?relid = 19623&hilite = .

9. Bruce Horovitz, "Fast-Food Restaurants Told to Warn of Addiction," *USA Today*, June 17, 2003.

10. Rick Mathieson, "Domino's Opens a Pizzeria in Your Pocket," *Mpulse Magazine*, August 2001, http://www.cooltown.com/ cooltown/mpulse/0801-commerce.asp.

11. Ibid.

12. Rick Mathieson, "Look Who's Talking Now: The New Revolution in Voice Portals & Services," *Mpulse Magazine*, September 2003.

13. Ibid.

14. Sue O'Keefe, "Ringback Tones Break Out in Song," *Telecommunications Magazine*, October 2003.

15. Jeff Leeds, "The Guy from Green Day Says He Has Your Mother on the Cell Phone," *New York Times*, August 18, 2004.

16. Olga Kharif, "America, Get Ready for 'Ringbacks,'" (citing Ovum projections), *Business Week*, June 25, 2004.

17. Reuters via *Wired News*, "Ring Tones Bringing in Big Bucks" (citing Arc Group projections), January 13, 2004.

18. Ibid.

19. Leeds, op. cit.

20. Zingy statement, August 2, 2004.

21. Ethan Smith, "Music Industry Struggles to Get Cellphone's Number," *Wall Street Journal*, September 13, 2004.

22. Rick Mathieson, "Two Thumbs Up: Hollywood's Hit Machine Goes Mobile," op. cit.

23. UPI, "Ringtones to Be Charted," June 1, 2004.

24. Rick Mathieson, "Personal Calls: Ringbacks Entertain Your Callers Before You Answer," *Mpulse Magazine*, August 2003, http://rickmathieson.com/articles/0703-ringbacks.html.

25. Nick Wingfield and Pui-Wing Tam, "Apple Rings Up Motorola to Play iTunes Songs on Cellphones," *Wall Street Journal*, July 27, 2004.

26. In-Stat MDR, "More Wireless Consumers Would Like to Tune In to Mobile Music Services," July 14, 2004.

27. *Business Week*, "America, Get Ready for 'Ringbacks,'" June 26, 2004, http://businessweek.com/technology/content/jun2004/tc20040628_0965_tc119.h tm.

28. Rick Mathieson, "Game Boy in the Crosshairs: The Serious Business Behind Wireless Games," *Mpulse Magazine*, July 2001, http://www.cooltown.com/cooltown/mpulse/0701-gaming.asp.

29. Ibid.

30. Rob Fahey, "Revealed—Sony's Wireless Network Plans for PSP and PS3," *GamesIndustry.biz*, May 4, 2004.

31. Clive Thompson, "The Making of an X-Box Warrior," *New York Times Magazine* August 22, 2004, p. 33.

32. Tom Loftus, "We Interrupt This Fantasy . . ." *MSNBC.com*, August 25, 2004. http://msnbc.msn.com/id/5722377/.

33. Olga Kharif and Stephen Baker, "Advertisers Take Aim at Gamers," *Business Week*, June 22, 2004, http://www.businessweek.com/technology/content/jun2004/tc20040622_2673_tc1 50.htm. The authors cite estimates from David Cole, president of gaming-market researcher DFC Intelligence San Diego.

34. Geoff Keighley, "Quick-Change Ads for the Joystick Generation," *Business 2.0*, August 18, 2004, http://www.business2.com/b2/web/articles/0,17863,681217,00.html.

CHAPTER FOUR

1. Jennifer Barrios, "Billboards that Know You," *New York Times*, December 14, 2003.

2. Ellen Neuborne, "Dude, Where's My Ad," *Inc. Magazine*, April 2004, p. 56.

3. Cynthia H. Cho, "Outdoor Ads, Here's Looking at You," *Wall Street Journal*, July 12, 2004. The author cites projections from ad-tracking firm TNS Media Intelligence/CMR.

4. Lisa Sanders, "Nielsen Outdoor Tracks Demo Data," *Advertising Age*, May 31, 2004, p. 14.

5. Andy Raskin, "Your Ad Could Be Here! (And Now We Can Tell

You Who'll See It)," *Business 2.0*, May 2003, http://www.business2
.com/b2/web/articles/0,17863,515629,00.html.

6. Cho, op. cit.

7. Jeanette Borzo, "Computer on Board, And It's Not a Laptop,"
New York Times, September 9, 2004.

8. Rick Mathieson, "The Fast & The Furious: Telematics and the
Converging Forces Driving the Car of Tomorrow," *Mpulse Magazine*, September 2001, http://www.cooltown.com/cooltown/
mpulse/0801-telematics.asp.

9. Ibid.

10. Ibid.

11. Ibid.

12. W. Daniel Garretson, "Voice Drives Telematics' Boom," Forrester
Research, with Carl D. Howe and Rebecca Shuman, June 2001,
http://www.forrester.com/ER/Research/Report/Summary/
0,1338,11125,FF.html.

13. Rick Mathieson, "Satellite Radio: Easy Listening or Treble
Ahead?" *Mpulse Magazine*, July 2002.

14. Rick Mathieson, "The Fast & The Furious: Telematics and the
Converging Forces Driving the Car of Tomorrow," op. cit.,
http://www.cooltown.com/cooltown/mpulse/0801-telematics
.asp. Author cites Peter Berggren, director of telematics for
Hewlett-Packard Company.

15. Ellen Neuborne, "Dude, Where's My Ad?" *Inc. Magazine*, April
2004. Author cites Arbitron as source of statistic.

16. Associated Press, "California Man Accused of Stalking via
GPS," *Los Angeles Times*, September 4, 2004.

17. Rick Mathieson, "The Fast & The Furious: Telematics and the
Converging Forces Driving the Car of Tomorrow," op. cit.,
http://www.cooltown.com/cooltown/mpulse/0801-telematics
.asp.

CHAPTER FIVE

1. Rick Mathieson, "Tag, You're It: Smart Tags, Intelligent Products, and the Race to Reinvent Retailing," *Mpulse Magazine*,

June 2002. http://www.cooltown.com/cooltown/mpulse/0602-autoid.asp.

2. Ibid.

3. Ibid.

4. ABI stance, July 2004.

5. In-Stat, "RFID Tags and Chips: Changing the World for Less than the Price of a Cup of Coffee," *Wireless Week*, January 12, 2005.

6. Jonathan Collins, "RFID Enters the Sports Arena," *RFID Journal*, July 30, 2004

7. Mathieson, op. cit.

8. Mathieson, op. cit.

9. Mathieson, op. cit. Author references comments by Jeffrey Jacobsen, CEO of Alien Technologies.

10. Mathieson, op. cit.

11. Mathieson, op cit. Author references Jeffrey Jacobsen, CEO of Alien Technologies.

12. Texas Instruments statement. http://www.ti.com/tiris/docs/solutions/epc/retail.shtml.

13. Mathieson, op. cit.

14. Bob Diddlebock, "Tags, You're It!" *Context Magazine*, February 2002, http://www.contextmag.com/archives/200202/feature 1tagsyoureit.as.

15. Phil Lempert, "We 'Check Out' Latest Supermarket 'Smart Court,' MSNBC, July 20, 2004.

16. Ian Austen, "Link-up in Aisle Four," *New York Times*, May 24, 2004, p C10.

17. Texas Instruments, "The Gap: In-Stock Inventory on the Sales Floor," corporate information, http://www.ti.com/tiris/docs/solutions/epc/retail.shtml.

18. Evan Schuman, "Coming Soon to a Retailer Near You: Custom Commercials," *eWeek*, December 29, 2004.

19. Rick Mathieson, "Targeted Audio: Message Bubbles, Sonic Guns and the Future of Sounds to Come," *Mpulse Magazine*, May 2003.

20. Suzanne Kantra Kirschner, "Audio's Next Big Thing?" *Popular*

Science Best of What's New 2002, September 20, 2002, http://www.popsci.com/popsci/science/article/0,12543,351353,00.html.

21. Debbie Gage and John McCormick, "Prada: The Science of Desire," *Baseline Magazine*, December 16, 2002, http://www.baselinemag.com/article2/0,1397,794142,00.asp.

22. Ted Fichuk, "The Electronic Product Code: RFID Reality," ACNielsen, *Consumer Insight Magazine*, Q4, 2003, http://10.190.20.95/acnielsen/pubs/documents/2003_q4_ci_electronic.pdf.

23. Rick Mathieson, "Shopping for Insights at the Store of the Future," *Mpulse Magazine*, August 2003, http://www.cooltown.com/cooltown/mpulse/0803-supermarket.asp.

24. Ibid.

25. Alorie Gilbert and Richard Shim, "Wal-Mart cancels 'smart shelf' trial," *Cnet News*, July 9, 2003, http://ecoustics-cnet.com.com/Wal-Mart+cancels+smart+shelf+trial/2100-1017_3-1023934.html.

26. Mathieson, "Shopping for Insights at The Store of the Future," op. cit.

27. Ibid.

28. Ibid.

29. Ibid.

CHAPTER SIX

1. Rick Mathieson, "The Wireless Hand that Feeds You," *Mpulse Magazine*, March 2002.

2. Ibid., http://www.hpbazaar.com/cooltown/mpulse/0302-restaurants.asp.

3. Corporate Web site, http://www.mcdonalds.com.

4. Jefferson Graham, "Businesses Cast Wi-Fi Lures to Hook Customers," *USA Today*, September 13, 2004.

5. Ecast, "Thousands of Broadband-Enabled Jukeboxes in Restaurants and Bars Nationwide to Provide Wireless Internet Access to Patrons," http://www.ipressroom.com/pr/ecast/info/broadband-jukeboxes-provide-wireless.asp.

6. Documentation from solutions provider HP.

7. Rick Mathieson, "Welcome to Hotel Tomorrow, Wireless Gadgets, Gateways and the Quest for the Ultimate Guest Experience," *Mpulse Magazine*, August 2002, http://www.cooltown.com/cooltown/mpulse/0802-hotels.asp.

8. Jeremy Rock, "Wireless POS Technology: Electronic Menu Systems Have Finally Arrived, *Hospitality Upgrade Magazine*, Spring 2004, http://www.hospitalityupgrade.com.

9. Mathieson, "Welcome to Hotel Tomorrow, Wireless Gadgets, Gateways, and the Quest for the Ultimate Guest Experience," op. cit.

10. Michael Kanellos, "Tech Spending to Rise in 2004, says IDC," *CNET*, December 4, 2003.

11. Debra D'Agostino, "Walt Disney Word Resorts and CRM Strategy," *CIO Insight*, December 2003.

12. Dawn Henthorn, "Your Pal and Mine . . . Mickey," *About.com,* "Florida for Visitors."

13. Debra D'Agostino, "Disney: Personalizing the Experience," *CIO Insight*, January 2004, http://www.cioinsight.com/article 2/0,1397,1476616,00.asp.

14. Rick Mathieson, "Learning's in the Air: Museums, Microcosms, and the Future of the Mobile Net," *Mpulse Magazine*, September 2001, http://www.cooltown.com/cooltown/mpulse/0901-museums.asp.

15. Jonathan Collins, "Lost and Found in Legoland," *RFID Journal*, April 28, 2004, http://www.rfidjournal.com/article/articleview/921/1/1/.

16. John Cook and Paul Nyhan, "Add Cell Phones to Trials of Flight," *Seattle Post Intelligencer*, September 21, 2004, http://seattlepi.nwsource.com/business/191723_mobile21.html.

17. Rick Mathieson, "The Wireless Web Goes Yahoo!" *Mpulse Magazine*, April 2002, http://www.hpbazaar.com/cooltown/mpulse/0402-christopherwu.asp.

18. Cook and Nyhan, op. cit., http://seattlepi.nwsource.com/business/191723_mobile21.html.

19. Rick Mathieson, "On a Wing and a Prayer," *Mpulse Magazine*, October 2001, http://www.cooltown.com/cooltown/mpulse/1001-traveler.asp.

20. Patty Donmoyer, "Delta Investing in Baggage Finder," *BT Online*, August 16 2004.

CHAPTER SEVEN

1. Lauren Etter, "Putting Tech to the Test," *Wall Street Journal*, September 13, 2004.
2. Strategy Analytics puts total data services revenue at $61 billion (August 17, 2004); IDC estimates that at least half of that is revenue based on messaging, versus games, ringtones, graphics, etc.
3. Helmut Meier, Roman Friedrich, and Hanno Blankenstein, "A Master Model for Mobile Multimedia," *Strategy + Business*, published by Booz Allen Hamilton, May 22, 2004.
4. *BBC News*, "Nokia Unveils Mid-Air Messaging," June 2, 2004.
5. Rick Mathieson, "The Mobile Web's New Mob Mentality," *Mpulse Magazine*, February 2003.
6. Erin Kandel, "A Mobile Link for 90 Mutual Friends," *New York Times*, May 13, 2004.
7. Lee Rainie, "The State of Blogging," Pew Internet & American Life Project, January 5, 2005, http://www.pewinternet.org/PPF/r/144/report_display.asp.
8. Pew Internet & American Life Project, press release, February 29, 2004.
9. Matthew Klam, "Fear and Laptops on the Campaign Trail," *New York Times Magazine*, September 26, 2004.
10. Steven Levy, "How Can I Sex Up This Blog Business," *Wired*, June 2004, http://www.wired.com/wired/archive/12.06/blog.html.
11. Rick Mathieson, "Small Pieces, Wirelessly Joined," *Mpulse Magazine*, December 2003, http://www.cooltown.com/cooltown/mpulse/1203-weinberger.asp.
12. Matt Hicks, "MSN Forms Search Focus Group," *eWeek*, September 30, 2004, http://www.eweek.com/article2/0,1759,1663788,00.asp.

13. David Kirkpatrick, "It's Hard to Manage if You Don't Blog," *Fortune Magazine*, October 4, 2004, http://www.fortune.com/fortune/technology/articles/0,15114,699971,00.html.

14. Thomas Mucha, "Have Blog Will Market," *Business 2.0*, September 30, 2004. http://www.business2.com/b2/web/articles/0,17863,703479,00.html.

15. Ibid.

16. David Carr, "At These Web Sites, It's a Man's World," *New York Times*, October 4, 2004.

17. Mucha, op. cit.

18. Sheryl Kay, "Tracking Down Adventure with Help of Technology," *Saint Petersburg Times*, October 31, 2003.

19. Bob Modersohn, "High-Tech Gadgets Help Hunt Easter Eggs," *Des Moines Register*, April 9, 2004.

20. Reuters, "'Toothing' Craze Goes Undergound," April 18, 2004.

21. Mark Ward, "Hide-and-Seek with Mobiles," *BBC News*, May 3, 2004.

22. Matthew Broersma, "Bluejacking" seen as marketing opportunity," *ZDNet UK*, December 4, 2003.

CHAPTER EIGHT

1. Kevin Maney, "Next Big Thing: The Web as Your Servant," *USA Today*, October 1, 2004.

2. Mark Ward, "Lifestyle 'Governs Mobile Choice,'" BBC News, December 8, 2004, http://news.bbc.co.uk/1/hi/technology/4071767.stm.

3. Maney, op. cit.

4. Rick Mathieson, "The Future According to Spielberg: Minority Report & The Future of Ubiquitous Computing," *Mpulse Magazine*, August 2002.

5. Peter Lewis, "Gadgets: Prose and Cons: Sony's New E-Book," *Fortune*, September 6, 2004, http://www.fortune.com/fortune/peterlewis/0,15704,685443,00.html.

6. Rachel Metz, "Changing at the Push of a Button," *Wired*, September 27, 2004.

7. Ibid.

8. Krysten Crawford, "Big Brother Says: Buy This!" *CNN Money*, September 2, 2004.

9. Barnaby J. Feder, "Technology Strains to Find Menace in the Crowd," *New York Times*, May 31, 2004.

10. Thomas J. Fitzgerald, "Fingerprints on File, Right from the Patrol Car," *New York Times*, September 23, 2004.

11. Kristen Gerencher, "Look This Way: ID Scans OK, Most Say," *CBS News Marketwatch*, January 8, 2003.

12. Ibid.

13. Susan Taylor, "Zarlink to Develop Medical Implant Antenna Chips," Reuters, via *USA Today.com*, July 13, 2004.

14. Rick Mathieson, "The Mobile Web's New Mob Mentality," *Mpulse Magazine*, February 2003, http://www.cooltown.com/cooltown/mpulse/0203-rheingold.asp.

15. Harry R. Webber, "Personal Info Breach Puts Data Warehouser in Hot Seat," Associated Press via *USA Today.com*, February 18, 2005, http://www.usatoday.com/tech/news/computersecurity/infotheft/2005-02-18-choice point-folo_x.htm.

16. Christopher Elliott, "Getting Off a Security Watch List Is the Hard Part," *New York Times*, November 2, 2004.

17. Steven Levy, "A Future with Nowhere to Hide?" *Newsweek*, June 7, 2004, http://www.msnbc.msn.com/id/5086975/site/newsweek/.

18. John Markoff, "Pentagon Plans a Computer System that Would Peek at Personal Data of Americans," New York Times, November 9, 2002.

19. Pentagon release on military contracts, November 12, 2002, http://www.defenselink.mil/contracts/2002/c11122002_ct577-02.html.

20. Scott Kirsner, "Chicago Moving to 'Smart' Surveillance Cameras," *New York Times*, September 21, 2004.

21. Associated Press via *CNN*, "Olympics' Digital Security Unprecedented," August 11, 2004.

22. Paul Elias, "Brain Scanners Can Probe Your Politics," Associated Press, October 28, 2004, http://msnbc.msn.com/id/6356637/.

23. Levy, op. cit.

A Glossary of mBranding
A Quick Reference Guide

3G   Third-generation mobile network. Fifty times faster than present-day cellular phone networks, delivers data at 144 kilobits per second—which is essential for video, music, Internet access, and more.

broadband   High-speed communications capable of delivering video, audio, and text at speeds of at least 144 kilobits per second.

bluetooth   A specification that allows for short-range wireless connections. With a range of about thirty feet, used to connect PCs to mobile phones or printers, and earpieces to phones.

BREW   Binary Runtime Environment for Wireless; a technology for delivering and displaying content to mobile phones.

carrier   A cellular service provider, à la Sprint PCS, Cingular, Verizon, and T-Mobile.

call-through   A prompt to initiate a cell phone call to a call center or sales office in response to a promotion.

cellular   Communications systems made of transmitters that divide a region into sections, or "cells." As the user of a cell phone moves between transmitters from one cell to another, his or her call travels from transmitter to transmitter uninterrupted. There are many forms of mobile/wireless communications called "cellular" by consumers, though the specifications and capabilities can vary widely.

click-through   Interaction with a mobile advertisement that leads to more information about a promotion.

e-wallet   A system that stores a customer's data—prepaid, credit card, or debit account information, for instance—to facilitate transactions electronically.

e-coupon   Coupons that are delivered electronically and that offer discounts or promotions. In wireless, these e-coupons can be scanned by special point-of-sale systems, or simply shown to a cashier at checkout.

frequency   The total number of times each marketing message is sent to each unique consumer.

GPRS   General Packet Radio Service: An efficient way to use limited bandwidth that is especially well-suited for sending and receiving data wirelessly, including e-mail, Web browsing, and large data packages.

GPS   The Global Positioning System, a constellation of twenty-four satellites that provides highly accurate data on a device's location; used extensively in car navigation solutions and, increasingly, for monitoring the location of children and elderly parents.

GSM   Global System for Mobile Communications. GSM is a digital mobile telephone system used in Europe and other parts of the world.

hot spot   An area where Wi-Fi service is available so you can wirelessly connect to the Internet; frequently offered in cafés, airports, and hotels.

i-mode   A proprietary mobile communications system launched by NTT DoCoMo that has enjoyed unprecedented success in

Japan and elsewhere because of its high-speed connectivity and services.

impression The transmission of a marketing message to a consumer. Total impressions = Reach × Frequency.

interstitials Advertisements that are inserted between wireline or wireless Web pages. According to mobile marketing firm Enpocket, proposed wireless standards include a 5-second fadeout and a skip feature.

Java A technology for delivering and displaying content to mobile phones.

l-commerce Location-based electronic commerce. This is e-commerce that responds to a customer's physical location. Examples include offers sent from a store whenever a consumer comes within a short distance.

M2M Machine-to-machine; the communication between machines over a mobile network. Could one day automate the delivery of content or services to specific devices. Example: music to your car stereo; or automated transactions based on preset preferences.

mBranding The strategic and tactical use of the mobile medium to create differentiation, generate sales, and build customer loyalty as never before possible.

m-commerce Mobile commerce; the use of mobile devices to conduct e-business.

MMS Multimedia Messaging Service. Enables mobile subscribers to exchange multimedia messages—any combination of text, picture, audio, video—via mobile device.

mobile Any form of communication or data transfer that takes place without wires.

mobile-fi Next-generation technology that extends high-speed wireless access to moving vehicles.

mobile IM Instant messaging, which offers real-time messaging with buddy lists, is increasingly being extended from the desktop Internet to the mobile world.

moblogging Mobile blogging. Creating and posting content—text, audio, picture, or video—to a Web log (or "blog") via wireless mobile device.

opt-in A policy whereby a customer gives explicit affirmation that he or she is open to receiving services or marketing messages delivered via a wireless mobile device. Variations include "double" or "confirmed" opt-in whereby a service or marketers send confirmation that a consumer has opted in for a service or marketing messages.

opt-out A policy whereby a customer has the choice to prevent content, services, or marketing messages from being delivered to their wireless mobile device.

pervasive computing Also referred to as "ubiquitous computing" or "ubicomp." Generally describes the trend toward the integration of computation into an environment in order to dynamically respond to people's needs, preferences, or directives transparently, often without any explicit interaction with a computing interface.

push advertising Generally refers to promotions sent to a consumer's wireless mobile device at a time other than when the consumer actively requests it.

pull advertising Generally refers to content and promotions sent to a consumer's wireless mobile device at the consumer's prompting.

reach The total number of unique consumers to which a marketing message is delivered.

RFID Radio Frequency Identification. Small RFID "smart tags" are tiny silicon chips that store data and a miniature antenna that enables the tag to communicate with networks. Could one day enable, for instance, frozen dinners that transmit cooking instructions to a microwave oven, or clothes that transmit cleaning instructions to a washing machine or dryer, or medicines that warn patients of dangerous interactions, among many other scenarios.

ringback   Sound bites that replace the traditional ringing sound a caller hears with a 30-second music clip or sound bite.

ringtone   Long the prime symbol of cell phone personalization; mono- and polyphonic sound bites that replace the standard ring of incoming calls with digital renditions of popular songs or voice clips, audible to all within earshot.

short code   An abbreviated telephone number, 4- to 5-digits, that can send or receive text messages.

SMS   Short Message Service; basically e-mail for mobile phones. Synonymous with "texting" and "text messaging."

spam   Unsolicited "junk" e-mail or SMS messages sent to large numbers of people to promote products or services.

spim   SPAM sent through instant messaging (IM), instead of e-mail or SMS systems.

telematics   The integration of wireless communications, monitoring systems, and location devices within a vehicle.

truetone   An actual music or sound clip used as either a ringtone or ringback, instead of a digital rendition. Also called a mastertone.

ultra-wideband   Connects your favorite toys—PCs, video cameras, stereos, TV sets, TiVo—at speeds 500 times faster than Bluetooth, and fifty times faster than Wi-Fi. Can be controversial because "UWB" signals are able to travel through building materials unobstructed, enabling police to peer through walls to monitor suspects and assess a hostage situation, among other military, rescue, and law-enforcement activities.

UMTS   Universal Mobile Telecommunications System. A third-generation (3G) mobile system that theoretically provides data speeds up to 2Mbps. That's enough to enable live color video on demand.

V-commerce   Voice-enabled electronic commerce; a computer's ability to interpret speech input and to respond and facilitate transactions using a prerecorded, often branded, voice.

viral marketing   A phenomenon in which consumers pass along marketing messages to a large number of friends, creating a snowball effect.

WAP   Wireless Application Protocol; a standard for accessing the Web from mobile devices. A WAP site is a wireless Web site.

Wi-Fi   Wireless Fidelity. An increasingly popular way to connect devices—PCs, printers, TVs—to the Net, and to each other, within a range of up to 300 feet.

WiMax   Long-distance Wi-Fi; can blanket areas more than a mile in radius to bring high-speed Internet access to homes and buildings too remote for traditional access.

wireless   Any form of communication or data transfer that takes place without wires.

wireline   A traditional wired phone line. Also called landline.

ZigBee   "Smart dust" technology that coordinates communications among thousands of tiny sensors, each about the size of a coin. Could one day be used for such things as managing a home, store, or office environment based on user's preferences, monitoring the toxicity of drinking water, and controlling remote diagnostics for home appliances, cars, and even humans.

Acknowledgments

It's true what they say: For such a solitary endeavor, no book ever gets written alone.

This project was made possible by the generous time and insights provided by many people quoted in these pages and some who are not. These include, but are by no means limited to: Linda Barrabe, Yankee Group; Justin Barocas, Anomaly; Gene Becker, Hewlett-Packard; Lars Becker, Flytxt; Hans-Gerd Bode, Volkswagen; Lauren Bigaleow; Carsten Boers, Flytxt; Andrew Bradbury, Aureole Las Vegas; Jack Braman, Venetian Hotel Las Vegas; Dave Buchko, BMW; Wes Bray, Hip Cricket; Steve Breighten, Gillette; Jeff Cohen, Aviation Software Group; Shawn Conahan; Michael Correletti, Dunkin Donuts; James Crawford; Dennis Crowley, Dodgeball; Paul Downes, Republic; Jaclyn Easton; Elgar Fleisch, University of Gallen's Institute of Technology Management; Rob Enderle, Enderle Group; Dan Engels; Avi Gardner, Jupiter Research; Rob Grimes, Accuvia; Lorraine Hadfield, Nielsen Outdoor; Scott Heintzeman, Carlson Hospitality; Carrie Himelfarb, Vindigo Studios; Craig Holland, Thumbworks; Lucy Hood, NewsCorp.; Chris Hoar, Textamerica; Harri Ihanainen, ZonePay, Inc.; Suzanne Kantra, *Popular Science*; Baruch Katz, Adapt Media; Larry Kellam,

Procter & Gamble; Tim Kindberg, Hewlett-Packard; Scott Lahman, Jamdat Mobile; Tom Langeland, Smart Sign Media; Joe Laszlo, Jupiter Research; Jonathon Linner, Enpocket; Brian Levin, Mobliss; Rachael McBrearty, IconNicholson; Alex McDowell; Phil Magney, Telematics Research Group; Tarun Malik, Hospitality College at Johnson and Wales University in Charleston; Jim Manis, m-Qube; Darla Marcomb; James Mastan, Microsoft; John Mayo-Smith, R/GA; Nihal Mehta, ipsh!; Erik Michielsen, ABI Research; Frank Nicholas, Wall Street District Hotel; Tom Nicholson, IconNicholson; Martin Nisenholtz, New York Times Digital; Elwood G. Norris, American Technology Corporation; Harriet Novet, Time Warner Cable of New York & New Jersey; Lanny Nguyn, L'anne; Amy O'Brien; Christine Overby, Forrester Research; Danielle Perry, AT&T Wireless; Barry Peters, Carat Interactive; Dr. Frank Joseph Pompei, Holosonic Research Labs, Inc.; Mike Popovic, Hiptop Nation; Chuck Porter, Crispin Porter + Bogusky; John Rickets, Ogilvy Asia/Pacific; Charles Robins, XM Satellite Radio; Dell Ross, InterContinental Hotels; Tim Rosta, MTV; Sanjay Sarma; Howard Sadel, North Carolina Hurricanes; Joel Schlader, DaimlerChrysler; Peter Schwartz, Global Business Network; Terrance Scott, Boeing Corp.; Larry Shapiro, Disney Interactive; Craig Shapiro, Proteus; Darren Siddall, GartnerG2; Ralph Simon, Mobile Entertainment Forum; Gary Stein, Jupiter Research; Michael Tchong, Trendscape; Albrecht von Truchsess, Metro AG; Brough Turner, NMS Communications; Marcello Typrin, Nuance; Lewis Ward, International Data Corporation; Stan Washington, McDonald's Corp.; David Weinberger; Russ Wilcox, E-Ink; Tom Williams, Wal-Mart; Lowell Winer, America Online; Christopher Wu, Yahoo Mobile; Christopher Young, J.P. Morgan Chase; Adam Zawel, Yankee Group.

I am especially grateful to Tom Peters, Don Peppers, Seth Godin, Christopher Locke, Gary Hamel, Howard Rheingold, and Chet Huber for taking time from their lives to be a part of this project. A special thanks to Tom, Don, and Seth (along with Jack Trout and Al Reis) for long ago inspiring me with radical ideas and changing the way I look at the business of marketing.

I would also like to thank Tom Antal, my colleague and friend, and a guy who really knows how to run a business. And Megan

Taylor (a.k.a. "M"), for always giving me free rein to pursue my particular brand of story. It's always a pleasure.

Thank you to my mother, Shirley, for teaching me the value of hard work; my late father, William, for encouraging my interest in reading and writing at a very young age; and my older brothers Glenn, Gary, and David, for teaching me how to take a pounding and still persevere. All of which prepared me for a career in advertising.

Thank you to Jim and Nora Stanton, for always encouraging me to ",Go for it!"

And many thanks to my acquisitions editor, Ellen Kadin, associate editor Mike Sivilli, copy editor Douglas Puchowski, proofreader Judy Lopatin, creative director Cathleen Ouderkirk, and the rest of the team at AMACOM Books, who have been a true pleasure to work with throughout this project.

Most important, a profound thank you to my wife, Judy, for her unwavering love, support, and patience during the four months I wrote this book—and for always believing. And finally, to my daughter, Kate, who has this writer unable to find even the simplest words to express how much she means to him. You are the loves of my life.

Index

About the Author

Rick Mathieson is an award-winning writer and media commentator on the worlds of marketing, media, and technology. His articles and commentaries have appeared in *ADWEEK, Mpulse,* and on National Public Radio. He also serves as vice president of creative strategy for Creative i Advertising & Interactive Media, one of Silicon Valley's most prominent advertising agencies.

Visit his Web site at: www.rickmathieson.com.

To continue the conversation on marketing's wireless revolution, visit: www.brandingunbound.com.